OFF-R ... IN THE EM. .S

Written and photographed by

Dariush Zandi

Published with the
support and encouragement
of Land Rover

MOTIVATE
PUBLISHING

Please protect the environment

Published by Motivate Publishing

Dubai: PO Box 2331, Dubai, UAE
Tel: (+971) 4 282 4060, fax: (+971) 4 282 0428
e-mail: books@motivate.ae   www.booksarabia.com

Office 508, Building No. 8, Dubai Media City, Dubai, UAE
Tel: (+971) 4 390 3550, fax: (+971) 4 390 4845

Abu Dhabi: PO Box 43072, Abu Dhabi, UAE
Tel: (+971) 2 677 2005, fax: (+971) 2 677 0124

London: Acre House, 11/15 William Road, London NW1 3ER
e-mail: motivateuk@motivate.ae

Directors: Obaid Humaid Al Tayer and Ian Fairservice

Edited by: Jackie Nel and David Steele

Design: Fredrick Dittlau and Johnson Machado

First published 1991
Reprinted 1993, 1994, 1995, 1996, 1998
Second edition 2002
Reprinted 2003, 2005, 2006

ISBN: 1 873544 20 0

British Library Cataloguing-in-Publication Data. A catalogue record for this book is available from the British Library.

Printed by Rashid Printers & Stationers, Ajman

Copyright in photographs Dariush Zandi with the exception of the following: Ronald Codrai p7:
OS Dais p47; Land Rover p23; David Steele p32, p115, p127, p135 and inside back cover.

CONTENTS

KEY TO MAPS

····················	Gravel road or track	🐚	Fossils
═══════	Tar road	🌳	Trees
════════	Dual carriageway	🐪	Camels
O O	Roundabout	⛽	Petrol station

Roads or tracks in red denote the route described in that particular chapter.

🏺	Archaeological site	📷	Photo opportunity
🛍	Shops	🏊	Swimming spot
⛰	Sand-dunes	⊷⊷⊷	Power lines
⛰	Mountain (*jebel*) peak	📡	Telecom tower
	Pools or puddles	E 1 44	Emirate highway number
◀	Dam	⇡	Distance marker
⤪	Bridge	*Suwalhat*	Village
⛺	Camp-site	**MADAM**	Town
♨	Picnic spot	**AIN ROAD 20km**	Distance to next town
🏛	Historical site	Madam N25°02.186' E55°48.507'	GPS co-ordinates
🏘	Settlement		
🌴	Oasis/farm		

The maps in this book are intended only as a guide to the routes described and do not purport to show international boundaries.

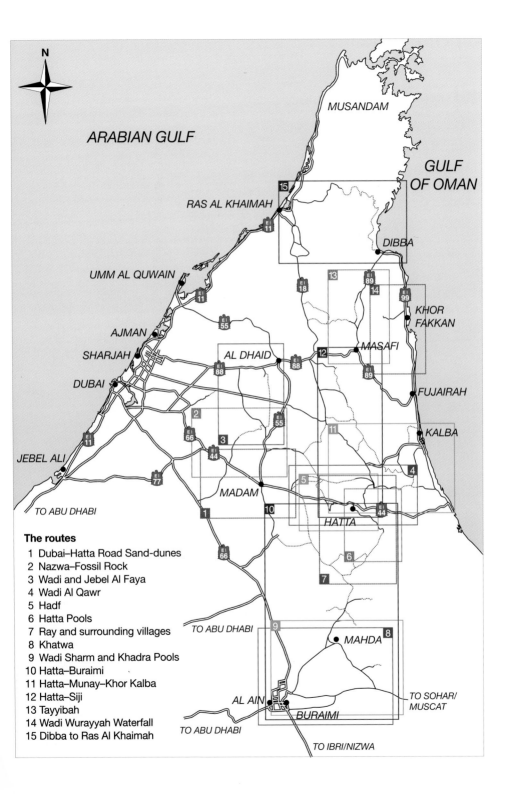

N

ARABIAN GULF

MUSANDAM

GULF OF OMAN

RAS AL KHAIMAH

DIBBA

UMM AL QUWAIN

KHOR FAKKAN

AJMAN

MASAFI

SHARJAH

AL DHAID

DUBAI

FUJAIRAH

JEBEL ALI

KALBA

MADAM

HATTA

TO ABU DHABI

The routes
1 Dubai–Hatta Road Sand-dunes
2 Nazwa–Fossil Rock
3 Wadi and Jebel Al Faya
4 Wadi Al Qawr
5 Hadf
6 Hatta Pools
7 Ray and surrounding villages
8 Khatwa
9 Wadi Sharm and Khadra Pools
10 Hatta–Buraimi
11 Hatta–Munay–Khor Kalba
12 Hatta–Siji
13 Tayyibah
14 Wadi Wurayyah Waterfall
15 Dibba to Ras Al Khaimah

TO ABU DHABI

MAHDA

AL AIN

BURAIMI

TO SOHAR/ MUSCAT

TO ABU DHABI

TO IBRI/NIZWA

FOREWORD

In the mid 20th century, when I lived in the UAE (or Trucial States, as they were then known), there were no roads, no frontiers and no security force. Few people of non-tribal origin travelled to the hinterland. Away from the coastal settlements travellers – such as the Bedu – had to be self-sufficient. They also had to tread warily into tribal territory, making certain that the armed retainers who accompanied them were of the correct tribal affiliation, since they were their 'passports' to safe-conduct.

On my return to the UAE in 1988, the whole region seemed much smaller than I recollected. This was the result of modern communications and the ease of travel which now made it practical to reckon distances in miles instead of travel time.

This contrast impressed me deeply and I am delighted to have been invited to introduce my friend Dariush Zandi's guide to off-road routes with a few words describing the nature of travel in the region during the time I lived there.

Of the many trips I made in and around the Hajar Mountains, the most memorable was a journey from Dubai to Muscat in the spring of 1948. Unlike my later journeys of that time, I had no independent means of transport or supplies, and was wholly reliant on the people I met *en route* for my food as well as transport and, not least, for my security.

I preferred to travel overland rather than by the suggested sea route and was introduced to the owner of a *bidfad*, the local name for a lorry, derived from ex-RAF Bedford trucks that had been disposed of on the market. As we started our journey I found myself perched precariously on the spare wheel as the vehicle lurched from side to side through the sand. It was a good position, better than the overheated and crowded cab and much better than the tightly-packed rear of the truck.

The truck's crew consisted of a driver-cum-mechanic, his assistant and general factotum, and the owner's son, who was responsible for negotiating a return load. Skins and tins of water were tied around the truck and a coffee pot suspended in an accessible position so that a brew could be prepared within minutes of stopping. There was no need for guards since more than half of the passengers were armed, and their rifles protruded from the truck at many angles.

Whenever the truck became stuck in the sand, everyone alighted and pushed it on its way to the top of a ridge, where it would stop for reboarding. At sunset we stopped on the sands near Jebel Faya, sharing with one another the various bits of food which some of us had brought for the trip and enjoying the communal coffee-pot, after which we slept on the still-warm sand, to awake to a cool, misty dawn. Before the mist had been cleared by a rapidly warming sun we were on our way to Wadi Al Qawr which, at that time, was the main pass through the mountains to the East Coast. After crossing a wide gravel plain, our transport slowly wended its way down and up out of the dry wadi bed and around large boulders, the cliffs on either side stopping any movement of air and making it increasingly hot.

The engine was overheating and the last of our drinking water was poured into the radiator. By the time we reached the small cluster of huts at Huwaylat (the first we had seen since leaving Dubai), it was clear that the lorry was in need of repairs.

We were lucky to have broken down in such a good spot. Water trickled through an open section of a *falaj* (irrigation channel), and we were able to refresh ourselves and take it in turns to share the shade of a small canopy of palm fronds built over it. The water was rather unpleasant to drink, but one of the passengers found small pools of sweet, winter rainwater in the hollows of nearby rocks. In the wadi, night and day were noticeably hotter than on the sands.

All in all, it took us 12 days to reach Muscat whereas, I am told, it takes about six hours on a good highway today!

Since my time in the Gulf many sand-dunes have been levelled by bulldozers and parts of the coastline have been reshaped by reclamation from the sea. But the distinctive outline of southeastern Arabia's spine, the Hajar Mountains, still looms through the morning mist.

In earlier times, the sparsely-scattered population of these mountains zealously guarded their meagre stocks of food and water and were highly suspicious of anyone who tried to enter their domain. But no one did, for there was no reason to do so, other than to use the few established passes linking the eastern and western coastal territories. Such was the often ill-deserved repute of the mountain dwellers that many travellers preferred to make their way round the peninsula by sea rather than through the mountains.

Nowadays, within the limitations of 4x4 vehicles – and individual enterprise and energies – the mountains are open to all to visit.

It's all too easy to become entrenched in the comforts and activities of town life, but, for anyone wishing to get away and explore the hinterland, perhaps to visit in a single day places which a few decades ago were inaccessible or unexplored, Dariush Zandi's book will serve as a useful guide and add interest to their excursions.

Ronald Codrai OBE
London, 1990

Wadi Al Qawr, circa 1950. For more information on this historic coast-to-coast route, turn to page 50 (photo: Ronald Codrai).

Introduction

The desert and mountains of the Northern Emirates afford some of the most interesting travelling and camping I've experienced during years of pursuing the great outdoors throughout the Middle East, Far East, Europe and North America. The natural beauty, wealth of history and sheer thrill of adventure and discovery make this region endlessly fascinating.

Most people are aware there's "something out there", but perhaps have never stopped to explore the hidden treasures of the countryside. Or they've never been initiated into the pleasures of camping or travelling off-road. I hope this book will encourage more people to learn about and enjoy their surroundings.

Much of the rural UAE is still unknown and unmarked and there are presently no detailed charts available to the public. The rough terrain and often hostile climate make the idea of a trip off the main road quite intimidating. But experience shows that a little effort will be rewarded.

This book offers the reader a cross-section of information including detailed route descriptions, GPS co-ordinates, notes on preparation for different kinds of trips (including vehicle preparation) and the camper's responsibilities. Included are detailed maps of each route featuring important landmarks, GPS co-ordinates, distances, names of relevant places etc.

The routes vary in length from half a day to a day and a half and may even be extended by combining various routes. I've been on camping trips in the northern and western regions of the Emirates that have lasted as long as 20 days.

The routes are presented regionwise, setting a starting point and defining subsequent checkpoints at various urban centres, easily reached by tarmac road, where off-road explorers and campers can replenish their rations before, during and after trips, as well as get their vehicles checked or make emergency stops.

As someone naturally curious about the heritage of this land, I have also set out to provide an insight into the traditional culture. Away from the urban centres, it's still possible to find village folk and mountain tribes following the old way of life, using traditional dwellings, apparel and indigenous handicrafts – which brings me to another point.

Since writing the original text more than 11 years ago there have been many changes, in keeping with the phenomenal pace of change in the UAE. These changes have naturally had a huge impact on the off-road routes and even the way of life of the rural villages.

Some routes that were nothing more than rough tracks through desert or mountains are now tarmac roads giving access to villages and towns. There are also well-hidden places that 10, even five, years

ago were accessible only to people on foot or on animals, but have now been opened to visitors by good access tracks or roads.

Another thing I've noticed in the last few years are more dry oases and dry farms, caused by a shortage of water, drought, over-farming and sinking of deep wells, as well as an increase in the population of the villages. Seeing water running in the wadis was one of the highlights of these trips; sadly, this is no longer so frequent a sight.

Another major change from the last book is the introduction and now common use of the Global Positioning System (GPS). As a writer, this has facilitated being able to pinpoint a precise location, important landmark or direction; for readers, it's made it far easier to follow routes and reach those previously hard-to-find places.

It also gives freedom and confidence in heading off on your own – and returning safely to your starting point.

In spite of all these changes, the places mentioned in the book are as interesting, rugged and natural as they've always been, and the people as interested, friendly and hospitable. As much as they've helped me to understand the roots of the people of the UAE, so they've helped other off-roaders appreciate the traditions and culture of the area.

I hope this fully updated edition of *Off-Road in the Emirates* will help, as the previous editions have done, in showing visitors and residents alike that there's far more to the desert than lifeless stretches of sand and barren mountains and that your off-road experiences will be as interesting as those I've had in researching, updating and photographing the various routes.

Dariush Zandi

In the UAE, the cooler months of mid-October to mid-May are the best for off-road exploring and camping, making seven months of comfortable adventure possible. While not impossible at other times of the year, the experience may not be as pleasant, although the writer has gone camping in July and August (the UAE's hottest months) and enjoyed these trips thoroughly.

Proper preparation and a little experience can minimise the difficulties of summer camping and your vehicle should obviously be air-conditioned and well-maintained to prevent overheating or any other problems along the way.

Confining your activities to the mountain tops, where there's a continuous breeze, or a shady oasis with running water and perhaps a pool in which to swim, reduces the impact of the heat. Unless you want to swim in the sea, areas away from the coast are more comfortable because of lower humidity. Naturally, selecting suitable tracks and camp-sites also helps.

Your vehicle

An important prerequisite for off-road driving is an appropriate vehicle, which

Enjoy travelling off-road with your children by following a few guidelines.

should be kept in tip-top condition. Problems can start if you keep a specific vehicle for this activity only, especially if it's left neglected and unserviced for months at a stretch when it's not being used. It's imperative that all vehicles get a thorough check-up before you head for the desert or mountains.

Chapter 2 is devoted to preparing and maintaining your vehicle. Your life could depend on it.

Planning a camping trip

Successful camping trips begin long before you lock your front door and drive away. The first few trips require more planning than subsequent ones, since it takes a little time to collect all the gear and establish a routine. For this reason, many people first take a few short 'practice' trips to establish camp-sites close to home. Doing this with experienced campers is especially helpful.

It's also recommended that you take copies of passports of all passengers and other identification such as labour cards, driving licences, health cards etc in case of an emergency.

Children

Off-road trips with children can be wonderful or dreadful and the difference is in the preparation. Babies can be the easiest to accommodate. A folding bed with mosquito netting makes a safe place for sleeping and playing, while a solid-framed papoose lets you take the baby everywhere with you. Pack plenty of drinking water for the baby, protect him or her from insects and the sun, and let the fresh air and family atmosphere take care of the rest.

Safety is the prime consideration for toddlers and young children. A play-pen

This camp-site is shaded by ghaf trees, neatly cropped by passing camels.

that doubles as a sleeping area is good. As youngsters tend to wander, a little bell pinned to the back of their clothing is an effective way of keeping track. Extra care is needed when the camp-site is near a road and a camp-fire should of course never be left unattended if youngsters are about. Don't forget plenty of changes of clothes.

Teenagers new to off-roading may well enjoy the challenge of navigating.

Children aged five to 11 make keen campers – they love new experiences and are enthusiastic, so let them participate and learn while they're helping. Board games, cards and books make good diversions. Precautions must be taken against children getting lost. It's a good idea to give each one a whistle to wear around their neck, with instructions to use them only in emergencies.

Older children and teenagers who have grown up on a diet of outdoor activity are more likely to accept a responsible role and take an active part in planning and preparation. Some become enthusiastic navigators and drivers. Teenagers new to off-roading may enjoy the challenge of navigating, exploring, and building and maintaining a camp-fire. Having children of a similar age to yours in the group is a good way to make sure they're kept fully occupied and enjoy their trip.

Destination

When deciding where to go, consider the distance and calculate how much time is required. Allow for plenty of time on the road so the driving can be part of the fun. Restrict the options to areas that offer activities you enjoy – such as mountain hiking or biking, exploring historical forts and watch-towers, photography, sightseeing, swimming in wadi pools or spending the day at the beach. Researching a destination is where the fun begins.

Getting ready to go

Develop a note-taking system to jot down all thoughts that come to you, starting with:

- Gear to take.
- Food to take (bearing in mind some items may be bought on the way or near the camp-site).
- Questions to ask about your proposed destination.
- Details for locking up the house.
- Clothing to pack.
- Vehicle check-up.

What to take

Be selective. When packing clothes, remember that temperatures can drop dramatically at night, and dew can dampen kit as thoroughly as if it had rained. Good footwear is essential if you intend to do a lot of walking and don't ever forget a hat.

You'll want direction-finding equipment such as compass, maps, binoculars, direction notes etc, especially if setting out over unfamiliar terrain. Nowadays a GPS (Global Positioning System) receiver is the best guarantee of finding your way.

Other staples of camping equipment include matches and flashlights of various sizes – a spotlight that works off a car battery is also good, while a miner's flashlight worn on the forehead will leave your hands free to carry out other activities. You can resort to candles if all else fails, so take a few along.

Sleeping accessories are matters of taste. For many people a sleeping bag is enough although a foam or blow-up mattress, even though bulky, is a valuable item, especially for sleeping in rocky wadis. Extra blankets during winter months are a wise precaution.

A tent is useful. It's always better to get a slightly larger tent than you think you'll need and a tent that provides both breathability (so moisture doesn't collect on the inside) and waterproofing is preferable. In this region, self-supporting tents such as dome tents – whose poles are pushed through sleeves on the outside of the tent to support it – are especially useful, as solid ground for tent pegs and guy ropes is not always available.

Metal pegs that are useful for mountainous terrain are too small for sandy ground and dune camping, so large plastic pegs are the best for this purpose. Put a lightweight groundsheet under your tent to protect it from sharp twigs and stones. It's always easier to clean a tarpaulin than a tent, and a piece of polythene works fine.

You might consider a camp-stove as more convenient than an open fire for cooking and warmth. With such items, the lighter the better. The writer usually carries different sizes of stoves: small ones

Camping at higher altitudes is cooler during the warmer months.

with rechargeable capsules for quick heating on a short camping trip and a Coleman two-burner fuel stove for an extended camping trip.

Your insulated icebox should have sturdy handles and hinges and a firm latch. Models with a bottom drain are handy. Two different-sized iceboxes, rather than one very large one, have the advantages of being easier to pack and carry, and can provide greater flexibility of storage and temperature control. A compact portable fridge, which works off a car battery, is very useful although somewhat expensive.

Using dry ice ensures your food will be kept dry. The writer usually freezes plastic water bottles prior to departing on a trip and uses them to keep the icebox cool and provide cool water throughout a journey. Storing various types of food in plastic containers before putting them in the icebox helps to keep them intact during rough journeys while specially-made items, such as plastic egg

containers, help to protect foodstuffs.

Folding tables and chairs are helpful but not essential. When selecting a table, make sure it's sturdy and there's no danger of its collapsing or tipping. The same goes for camp-chairs.

All-purpose tools to take along include a pocket knife (or, better still, a Swiss Army knife or a Leatherman) and a hatchet and shovel are a must. In the dunes, shovels of various sizes are the tools you may need to dig your vehicle out of the sand if it gets stuck. A loud whistle is also handy as a precaution against getting lost or separated from your party. Your personal items might include a first-aid kit, suntan lotion, sewing kit, safety pins, string and nylon cord.

There are numerous gadgets you can take along but experience will teach you what's really essential. Here's a list to help you on your way:

Pack selectively for camping, but take all the essentials you'll need.

Vehicle and general equipment

- One or more spare tyres.
- Tyre-pressure gauge.
- Tyre-repair kit.
- Electrical-control winch.
- First-aid kit.
- Fire extinguisher.
- Shovels.
- Towing rope, chain and shackles, industrial-type gloves.
- High-lift or other type jack (which can also be used as a winch), wheel brace, base plate.
- Five-foot aluminium ladder (for use as a sand ladder).
- Air compressor.
- Hammer, crowbar, axe.
- Powerful hand lamp operated from socket for vehicle cigarette lighter.
- Air bag.
- Length of rope for general use.
- Basic tool kit, screwdrivers, insulated pliers, insulation tape, masking tape, spanners, spare sparkplugs and plug spanner, Stanley knife or similar, insulated wire for electrical connections, roll of strong cord, jump-leads, can of WD40 etc.
- Sheet of thick plastic, sacking or tarpaulin about 2x2 metres. This can be used under the wheel for traction, or to lie on if working under the vehicle, or for shade.
- Length of plastic or rubber hose – useful for siphoning petrol from one tank to another.
- Large torch and batteries.
- Strap/stretch cords and plastic ties.
- Extra fluids and oil for various vehicle parts.
- Extra fuel, bulbs and wires of different types, and jump leads.
- Fan belt and radiator hose.

Personal items

- Toothbrush, toothpaste, toiletries.
- Candles and/or small torch, batteries.

Getting back to camping basics in the desert wilderness of the UAE.

- Matches or lighter.
- Insect repellent.
- Binoculars.
- Whistle.
- Extra clothing and hiking shoes.
- Food (depending on trip duration).
- Water.
- Maps, compass, GPS receiver.
- Mobile phone and/or satellite phone.
- Swiss Army knife or Leatherman.
- Pen and pencil, notebook.
- Swimsuit and towel.
- Sun-glasses, and sun-protection lotion with a high SPF.
- Camera, tripod and film.
- Waterproof bag.

Camp-site items

- Tent.
- Sleeping-bags or blankets.
- Roll-up mattresses.

- Groundsheet or mats.
- Pillows or cushions.
- Folding table and chairs/stools.
- Gas or battery lamps.
- Cool-box.
- Compact camp-stove.
- Two-burner stove fuel.
- Barbecue grid.
- Garbage bags.
- Charcoal, fire-lighters.
- Cutlery, tongs, tin opener, corkscrew, cutting knife.
- Plates, spoons, mugs.
- Frying pan, pots, pans, kettle.
- Washing-up cloth and liquid, soap.
- Kitchen-paper roll, tea towels.
- Wet wipes.
- Cutting board.
- Spare water supply for cooking and washing.
- Solar-heated bag shower.
- Aluminium foil.

Dome tents are better suited to local conditions than other types.

Packing

Use a check-list to guide you through the packing process and remind you what must be taken. Pack clothes in plastic bags, which can be squeezed in between other items, and keep a few extra plastic bags with you. Stuff sleeping-bags inside their own packing bags. Most of the gear should be packed in its original box if possible. Gather everything you're taking: clothing, sleeping items, kitchen equipment, camping gear, handy travel items and so on to get a visual image of it.

Organise all food, except items for the icebox, with the rest of the gear. Take a good look at everything, think it through and check what you see against your list. Set aside the items that need to be accessible. Load the items, not according to categories, but according to size and weight, always keeping in mind the principle: "Last in, first out".

Always remember to pack your vehicle tools where they can be most easily reached. Just before you leave, fill the

icebox and load it into your 4x4.

Having one or two lockable plastic boxes to permanently store vehicle-maintenance tools and camping, cooking and sleeping gear will help to speed up packing and ensure a hassle-free trip. You can pre-pack almost all your gear except perishable food.

At the camp-site

Plan to arrive during daylight hours, allowing time to put up your tent, unpack and organise things. Setting up the tent is something the whole family can do together. The children will soon learn how to do the job, which can also be a lot of fun.

Before setting up the tent check the slope of the ground and establish your camp away from any water run-off. Find a spot where the tent can be in the shade during the heat of the day and try to position it a safe distance from the fireplace.

Clear away rocks or any other obstructions – especially thorns – from your chosen site and put a small rug or straw mat in front of the tent to keep the interior and the bedding clean.

Organise your kitchen, cooking gear and food for maximum convenience. Place the icebox in the shade and keep the fuel canisters away from the fire. Set up your garbage bag. If you're using a plastic bag, it can be tied around a nearby tree with a piece of rope, leaving an opening in the bag for filling it. Your lantern can be hung from a rope or moved around as needed.

The camp-fire

If there's one traditional symbol of camping, it's the camp-fire. Nevertheless, don't make a huge fire unless it's made from wood that you've brought with you. Wood in the UAE is scarce and it's environmentally incorrect to gather wood that's so valuable to the creatures of the desert. Don't waste wood just to impress your friends – rather take wood or charcoal with you.

Always remember to keep an eye on the children around the fire and never put empty fuel canisters in the fire or use petrol to light a fire.

Charcoal for cooking can be selected as required and placed in a separate heap in a shallow ditch surrounded by evenly arranged flat rocks large enough for your steel (stainless steel is preferred) grid. Premarinated meat is recommended.

If you find a neatly cut and piled stack of wood don't touch it. It has most likely been cut and prepared by nearby villagers for cooking and, not surprisingly, they can get quite offended if you use their wood.

Fire making is a skill. Stack kindling (paper, leaves, twigs, small branches and well-split logs) over the tinder so that it's arranged in a circle and leans together at the top to form a small pyramid. Light the fire at the bottom of the tinder. Always light it upwind, that is, with the wind blowing the match flame into the tinder. As the pyramid burns, it will light the surrounding charcoal.

Remember, no matches or lighter – no camp-fire.

Camp-ground etiquette

Campers often share the same territory, so group cooperation is essential. Don't

It's environmentally friendly to take firewood or charcoal into the desert.

Prepare food – such as the mixture for these flapjacks – before you leave home.

pollute a stream or *falaj* (water channel) and don't clean fish or wash clothes in the water. Dig a pit when you need to go to the toilet and light the paper once you've finished. Be quiet at night and in the early hours of the morning and rather enjoy the sounds of nature than a blaring radio or CD player. Don't gather firewood from the desert and never chop or pull down a branch of a live tree or mutilate shrubs or trees. Gather all your garbage in a bag and take it home with you. Before leaving the camp-site ensure that it's clean, even if this means taking other peoples' rubbish with you. Remember the golden rule: take only photographs, leave only footprints.

Food for a camping trip

The type of food you choose for a trip depends on individual taste but here follow a few general hints.

Canned food is convenient to pack and can be prepared and heated without a fuss. Alternatives include homemade sandwiches, salad, fruit and tinned drinks. Some people prefer to take cold meat and salads and like to prepare their sandwiches on the spot. Others look forward to a barbecue with meat, chicken or fish, even though this usually takes more time to prepare and clean up afterwards.

If you know you'll be on the move constantly, sandwiches might be your best bet. Food should be packed in well-sealed, proper containers for protection, to keep it as fresh as possible and to prevent spillage. Meal-sized containers are useful to ensure you don't over-pack for a short trip.

Plan your meals well in advance so you'll have everything you need. Think about what you need and what your family likes – and consider its preparation. Camping makes everyone hungry. Some welcome camping snacks are small boxes of juice, carrot and celery sticks, raisins, nuts, corn chips, crackers, cheese and quartered peanut-butter sandwiches.

Your icebox will stay cooler longer if you start out with contents that are as cold as possible. Items that can be frozen ahead of time and then stored in the icebox include meat, cheese, fruit juice in cardboard containers and water. The

Familiarise yourself with the territory before you set out to explore it.

icebox will probably need fresh ice daily. For maximum efficiency, open the icebox as little as possible, and keep it covered and in the shade.

One way to simplify food preparation during camping is to prepare some food in advance. Bread and desserts are two suitable items, ready to enjoy at any time, while dried food will give you a head start on your camping trips.

If you are into outdoor cooking, you could use one of these three methods:

Foil cooking: Choosing the right kind of coals is important here. A blazing fire will not do, so start your fire well ahead of the cooking time to allow it to die down to glowing embers. Charcoal can be used as a base; hot coals alone are too hot. Mix them with ashes to temper the heat.

Spread out two or three thicknesses of foil and coat the top surface with margarine, butter or oil to prevent the food from sticking to it. Place your food on the greased foil and wrap it carefully. Seal (crimp) the edges securely. Make a second wrap that covers the seal with a smooth covering. Shovel the coals aside, then lay the foil-wrapped food on the hot ashes and coals. After the food has cooked for the recommended time, remove with a pair of barbecue tongs. Beware of escaping steam when you open the package.

There are several local dishes that can be prepared in this way, such as ghoozl with lamb meat. Corn-on-the-cob, potatoes and mixed vegetables are also excellent when cooked in this manner – make sure you include butter and seasonings inside the foil.

Open-fire cooking: Stay warm and cook your food on a stick or skewer at the same time. This gives the true feeling of camping. Use a light, straight green stick, or a cooking fork or kebab skewer. Peel the sticks at the cooking end. You can use them to cook a hot dog over the fire, or a piece of bread for breakfast or as barbecue toast.

Barbecue: This is perfect for camping so don't forget to take a grill with you. Once you've finished with the grill, pack it in a paper bag or wrap it in newspaper and put this parcel into a plastic garbage bag to prevent it from soiling other gear.

Finding your way

Familiarise yourself with the territory before you set out to explore the wilderness. Study the maps in this book or any other maps you have. Find out where the main roads, side roads and tracks are. Check the wadis: which way do they flow and to what main wadi do they lead; where are the main ridges and which way do they lie?

In the field (especially in dune areas), high ground may give a good view of the area and will help to identify any landmarks in the territory around you. See that the road you're following tallies with the route on your map. Tracks often follow wadi courses, which makes them easier to keep in sight. Use your compass, and record the distance between main changes in direction. Where the road passes any distinct feature such as a hill, dune, stream confluence or tree, stop to confirm the location and correct your plotting if necessary.

When you come to a point where you propose to leave the vehicle and continue on foot, determine on the map the maximum perimeters of the ground you may cover.

Orientation with a map

A map is simply a picture to scale of what exists on the ground. Water courses, roads, wadis, mountains, desert, power lines and other structures are represented by lines and symbols which will be defined, along with the scale, on the map. Vertical relief (ie the contours of wadis and ridges) is defined by contour lines.

All that's required to develop adequate skill in interpreting these symbols, particularly the contour lines, is practice

in the field. The writer finds it useful to orient the map so that details coincide with the landscape. Then stand on whichever side of the map lets you look out over it to the features of the landscape you wish to identity.

Also, keep the scale in mind. If a feature is clearly many miles away, it's going to be some distance away on the map too. Make the best estimate you can and then search in the right direction at that distance on the map, according to the scale.

Using a compass

A compass will show you magnetic north as long as you use it away from other magnetic influences. To determine with a high degree of accuracy any direction, you need to adjust your reading for true north. The magnetic declination in the UAE is 1°49'.

Position yourself on the opposite side of the compass to the line of travel. Once you've determined on the map the direction that will take you from your present location to your destination, you'll know which way to drive so as to travel on that bearing. A good way of holding your course is to line up a distant feature of the landscape and head toward it. You can stop occasionally to check your heading.

What is GPS?

The Global Positioning System (GPS) is a satellite-based navigation system made up of a network of 24 satellites placed into orbit. GPS works in any weather conditions, anywhere in the world, 24 hours a day. There are no subscription fees or set-up charges to use GPS.

How it works

GPS satellites circle the earth twice a day in a very precise orbit and transmit signal

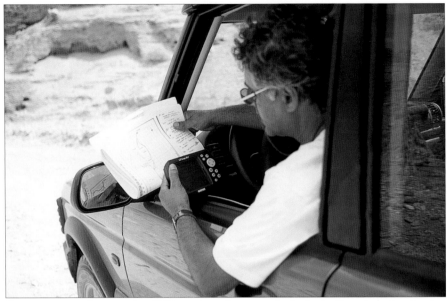

In recent years inexpensive GPS receivers have revolutionised off-road navigation.

information back to earth.

GPS services take this information and use triangulation to calculate the user's exact location. Essentially, the GPS receiver compares the time a signal was transmitted by a satellite with the time it was received. The time difference tells the GPS receiver how far away the satellite is. Now, with distance measurements from a few more satellites, the receiver can determine the user's position and display it on the unit's electronic map.

A GPS receiver must be locked on to the signal of at least three satellites to calculate a 2D position (latitude and longitude) and track movement. With four or more satellites in view, the receiver can determine the user's 3D position (latitude, longitude and altitude). Once the user's position has been determined, the GPS receiver can calculate other information such as speed, trip distance, distance to destination,

sunrise and sunset time and more.

Today's GPS receivers are extremely accurate. Although certain atmospheric factors and other sources of error can affect their accuracy, most receivers are accurate to within 10–15 metres.

Both hand-held models and models designed to be fitted in vehicles are available on the market.

GPS satellites transmit two low-power radio signals, which travel by line of sight, which means they'll pass through cloud, glass and plastic but will not go through most solid objects in the vicinity, such as buildings and mountains.

Most GPS receivers can display positions in various position formats. The format used in this book is to present latitude and longitude in degrees, minutes and thousandths of a minute (hddd°mm.mmm'), the default format in Garmin GPS receivers. Make sure these co-ordinates match those on your own GPS receiver and maps.

Preparing and Driving Your Vehicle

The first part of this chapter is a brief introduction to optimal management of vehicles in desert conditions, taken from *Expedition Planners' Handbook and Directory* (Expedition Advisory Centre, London).

The second part of the chapter contains useful and practical advice based on the writer's experience. . . .

Guidelines for off-road driving

The brevity of these guidelines should not be taken as encouragement for the inexperienced to underestimate the high standard of driving and preparation needed for exploring wadis and driving on dunes or mountain tracks.

Equipment

Packing: Thorough, rattle-free packing of equipment not only ensures its safety and durability but also allows the driver to feel easy and comfortable at the wheel. A rattle-free vehicle tends to be driven well and a vehicle driven smoothly and sympathetically lasts longer.

Vehicle-recovery equipment: Two shovels per vehicle. Five-foot, close-runged aluminium ladders (sand ladders) are excellent for putting under the wheels when you bog down in soft sand. They are light and effective and you may have to use them repeatedly to get through a long soft patch, picking them up and running in front of the vehicle to lay them before the wheels again.

In bad static bogging, do not skimp on the digging – five minutes more with the shovel before restarting the engine can be well worth the effort if it results in first-time extraction.

A really long tow-rope – about 50 metres – with a second vehicle and coordinated clutchwork on the towed and towing vehicles is best. People pushing are far more effective than you'd expect. Lower tyre pressure as recommended but make sure you reinflate the tyres as soon as conditions permit.

Vehicles

Route and transmission: The terrain to be encountered on the route governs choice of vehicles with four-wheel-drive

Proper preparation and maintenance will ensure safe, enjoyable off-road adventures.

(4x4) or two-wheel-drive (4x2). On tracks, for example, you may get by with a rugged 4x2 vehicle. Off tracks anywhere, take a 4x4.

Petrol versus diesel: Fuel availability *en route* can affect this but not often; although kilometres per gallon and overall fuel costs favour diesel, the preference in the Gulf is for petrol. Diesels are heavier with less power output than equivalent petrol-engine vehicles, but have a very wide torque band for slogging in deep sand.

Oil: The basic functions of an engine oil are to cool, clean and protect the engine. There are specially manufactured engine oils developed with special base oils and additives to ensure better viscosity and superior engine protection. Off-road vehicles require these oils because of the rough terrain and driving conditions they have to negotiate.

Ask your trusted mechanic. Find out how an ideal combination of the right selection of engine oil, gear oil, brake fluid, grease and coolants can synchronise a consistent high performance. By using the right mix you may even be able to reduce fuel consumption.

Make sure you change the engine oil according to your vehicle manufacturer's recommended specifications and check for any leakages at the same time, that you check the level of engine oils before you embark on a journey.

Tyres: Be fastidious about tyre pressure. As a guide, use the manufacturer's recommended road pressures on rock and stones, 75 per cent of this on/off road, and 50 per cent on very soft sand. Drive slowly at sand pressures on deflated tyres to avoid overheating them. Reinflate when on hard ground. Be careful not to damage sidewalls on rocks and stones.

Vehicle spares: You can't take everything so restrict your list to non-repairable items over which you have no control.

The need for spares is most often caused by poor driving, so drive carefully to safeguard your suspension and transmission. Concentrate on fuel pumps and filters, fan belts and hoses, small non-repairable electrical items such as coil, condenser and points. Take lots of 'botching' kit – Araldite, Hermetite, rolls of tape, selection of jubilee clips, nuts, bolts etc. And always bear in mind a thorough pre-expedition service is better than a big box of spares.

Tools: Know your vehicle and take only what's needed. There's no shortcut to devising a tool kit and knowing your vehicle is the key factor. Include two good jacks (and a small square of wood to prevent them from sinking into the sand). Include a good set of jump leads.

Loading: Never overload. On 4x2 vehicles try for not more than 75 per cent permitted payload if you're planning much rough going. If you use a roof-rack, keep the load to within manufacturer's recommended limits.

Maintenance: Since the vehicle is your lifeline, treat it accordingly. Check levels in the morning when the engine is cool.

Driving: Drive gently and sympathetically. There are hundreds of rules but the most important are:

- Never spin the wheels when you start to bog down in soft sand – if you do, the tyres will act like milling cutters to scoop out ground until you are resting on the chassis.
- Know when to quit and reverse out – a proud driver is one who generally does a lot of digging and earns the undying irritation of his peers.
- Anticipate and use the correct gear to avoid unnecessary gear changing in difficult sand conditions. In general, high range will give best results in sand but judicious use of low range may be required in the heaviest going. Descents should a

Engine protection proven in the extreme.

اقصى حماية
في كل أحوال القيادة
Superior protection
in all driving conditions

زيت محركات نصف مُخَلِّق صناعياً
SYNTHETIC TECHNOLOGY MOTOR OIL   15W-50

Shell
HELIX

always be undertaken in a range and gear that provide adequate engine braking to avoid use of brakes.

- Reduce tyre pressure in difficult going and reinflate when conditions permit. Don't drive too close to the vehicle in front – it may need space to reverse out of a tricky situation.

Fuel and Water

Fuel: Metal jerry cans are the best choice because they're extremely safe as well as being easy to handle.

How much should you carry? It's as vital to carry sufficient fuel and reserves in the desert as it is not to overload the vehicle. Fuelling points are invariably widely spaced; the distance between them is a major criterion in selection of vehicle, total payload left over for the crew and other supplies. If 'D' is the distance between fuelling points: total gallons required = (D + 25 per cent + 150 kilometres) divided by expected kilometres per gallon (ie a reserve of 25 per cent plus 150 miles to cover diversions and difficult going).

Distance: Away from tracks (eg an expedition reaches a base supply town and then branches out across the country), D will be a distance measured off a map. Factor it according to terrain; on a big map (1: 1 m, say) actual distance will be about 1.2 times measured distance, given reasonable going such as gravel and some stony regions. Savannah, slow going with much zigzagging between grass tussocks, will be 1.3; sand dunes 1.5 to 2; and smooth sand/gravel plain 1.1.

Fuel accounting: It's essential to do a nightly calculation of your fuel consumption and check fuel remaining in

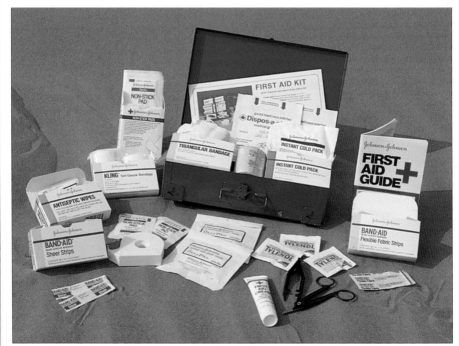

A good first-aid kit is an important accessory for any off-road vehicle.

THE FINEST PERFORMANCES ARE THOSE THAT LAST

MICHELIN
4X4 SYNCHRONE
TYRE

OUTSTANDING PERFORMANCE
ON ROADS AND TRAILS,

SAFETY, COMFORT,

ENDURANCE AND MILEAGE.

*A versatile tyre which ensures safe driving
in both dry and wet roads and still
delivers good performance off road*

MICHELIN

tanks and cans. Know exactly the amount used to top up each night and divide it into the distance covered.

Water: Hard polythene military-like jerry cans are unsurpassed for normal use. For one or two days, a cooler filled with ice can be topped up as required.

Experience over a number of expeditions shows water requirement at low physical workloads is 7.5 to 10 litres per head per day with night/day min/max 5–35°C; 12.5 to 20 litres per head per day with night/day min/max 25–45°C.

For how many days does this hold true? There are no hard and fast rules, but a minimum of three extra days' worth is a prudent reserve to cover, say, time-consuming breakdown repair work. Thus a journey involving six days of travel would need a nine-day supply of water.

Tips from a frequent off-roader's notebook

For frequent off-road travellers, preparing a vehicle involves more than just a simple servicing, but it pays off. The writer has used the same mechanic for a number of years and explains to him what's required of his vehicle and what kind of terrain he expects to encounter – also bearing in mind that all the trips in this book, and probably most others you'll do in the Emirates, include some highway driving as well as off-road routes.

Tyres are always the starting point. Check the pressure, the wear and tear, and the balance. Include your spare in all stringent checks. For a long, tough journey, you might be wise to include two spares. Manufacturers will recommend a certain pressure for asphalt roads; lower pressures are recommended for desert driving, and higher for mountain driving. A manual or mechanical air compressor, with a pressure gauge, is a highly recommended tool to take with you.

Any irregular or unusual sounds

coming from under the bonnet should be checked out thoroughly. Likewise, your servicing should ensure all oil seals and the entire car are checked for oil leakage. Brakes and clutch-fluid levels should also be checked.

All nuts and bolts should be tightened and all caps (radiators, battery, brake and clutch fluid etc) should be properly secured. When the going gets tough any of these could be shaken loose and drop off.

The vehicle suspension and the shock absorbers are other important parts that require checking to ensure they are up to the rigours of rocky mountain roads or desert sand. The electrical parts and wiring should be examined and repaired if necessary. Exhaust pipes and the silencer are some parts that can take a battering. Check them carefully, especially if you've been off-roading recently.

It's important to carry some tools and spares with you. Experience has shown that an extra fan belt, brake and transmission fluid and radiator coolant are musts in the general-repair kit. You'll know best what other spares you may need for your own vehicle.

Running checks

Tyres should be checked before and after driving off-road for damages and signs of wear and tear. You can do this as a matter of course when you adjust tyre pressures. A quick check under the car and under the bonnet is a wise precaution. You'll often find that something has worked itself loose or come off while you were negotiating rocky tracks. Prompt attention to such defects may avoid accidents and costly repairs later.

Off-road driving is generally more risky than on-road driving. A driver must be vigilant at all times. The condition of the track must be constantly monitored to avoid obstructions and hazards. Take extra care whenever you drive off established tracks, and use extreme caution when driving on a damaged or obscure track, especially at the blind spot on the crest of a hill. Generally, driving slowly can save you from nasty accidents and give you enough time to cope with any serious situations.

Proceed on foot

Everyone should get out of the vehicle before the driver negotiates a dangerous section of the track. One person can easily guide the driver over the difficult stretch. In such situations every movement of the vehicle and tyres should be closely watched. Sometimes it may be necessary to smooth or build up the track before proceeding – whether you push on or retrace your route sometimes depends on how adventurous and imaginative you are!

At the start of a steep incline, be sure to check the brakes and the steering and, if you have a low-ratio gear, use it to reduce the pressure on the engine and brakes. Before you attempt going down a steep hill be sure that your vehicle is able to make the journey back up again. Don't forget that it's always easier for a vehicle to climb a hill when its load is light.

Speed, a blind curve and a change in the characteristics of the road caused this.

ROUTE 1 DUBAI–HATTA ROAD SAND-DUNES

This is a comparatively short trip, with its starting point conveniently about 30 minute's drive from Dubai. The area boasts some of the highest sand-dunes in the region, spread over a wide area and reaching 275m above sea level. It's an ideal choice for climbing dunes and 4x4 driving – especially if you possess a dune buggy. (Dune buggies – or quad bikes – are available for rent at the destination.)

The rolling red dunes also make this area a special favourite with artists and photographers. Scenes at sunrise and sunset, with the interplay of smooth curves and shadows, are irresistible.

IN BRIEF

STARTING POINTS: Dubai or Sharjah/Al Hibab Roundabout.

FINISHING POINTS: Dubai or Sharjah/Al Hibab Roundabout.

DISTANCE: 15km, excluding side trips, from Al Hibab Roundabout to the entrance to the main Hatta Road Sand-Dune fields.

TIME REQUIRED: Half a day.

CATEGORY: Saloon car. A 4x4 vehicle or dune buggy is needed if any sand driving is intended.

HIGHLIGHTS: High sand-dunes, desert-sand driving, camping and photographic opportunities.

How to get there

The Dubai–Hatta dual carriageway takes you directly to the dunes alongside this superb road, a convenient 30-minute's drive from Dubai. The route takes you past Awir, Al Hibab Roundabout and the Nazwa Junction.

At Al Hibab Roundabout, zero your odometer (N25°02.135' E55°35.486'). There's a petrol station and shops immediately beyond the roundabout, where you can replenish fuel, water and foodstuffs. Adjustments to your tyre pressures can be done here too. Closer to the dunes, the Nazwa Junction (8.2km) offers the same

There are some magnificent sand dunes about 30 minutes' drive from Dubai.

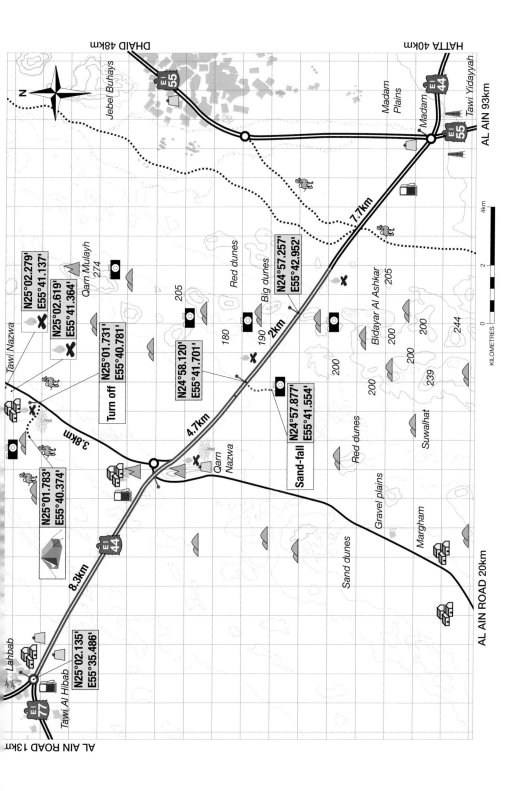

facilities but is usually more crowded.

The main Hatta Road Sand-dunes start 15km from Al Hibab Roundabout and can be easily observed on either side of the road (N24°57.257' E55°42.952'). The colour of the dunes changes to red immediately beyond Al Hibab and remains uniformly red until you reach your destination.

An interesting feature along the way is Qarn Nazwa (8.3km/N24°59.925' E55°39.680'). In Arabic, *qarn* means 'outcrop' and this one, which stands half covered in sand, contains fossils of seashells and other marine life, indicating the area was once covered by the sea or moved here during the continental drift. There are actually outcrops, known as Quroun (plural of *Qarn*) Nazwa, on both sides of the road.

Another interesting side trip is a visit to the sandfall situated in a sand quarry. To reach this, turn right (southwards) at 13km (N24°58.120' E55°41.701'). Drive for 500m down into the quarry. If the sand is

freshly excavated (a couple of days to a week before your visit), and if there's enough wind to push the sand over the top, you'll see a sandfall resembling a waterfall, with an intriguing mix of colour and form that'll make it hard to put your camera down (N24°57.877' E55°41.554').

Once back on the road continue your trip towards the main dunes (15km), to a spot where you can hire dune buggies (quad bikes), motor bikes and go on camel rides. (Please note that unless specified the distances indicated in brackets do not include any detours.)

The sand-dunes run from north to south on either side of the road. If you're on foot you should climb to the top of the nearest dune from where you'll get a magnificent view of the whole area.

If you have a 4x4, however, travel 8km northwards in the direction of Qarn

When conditions are right, you can see a sandfall near Qarn Nazwa.

Dune driving is a test of your skills and your vehicle's performance.

DESERT PLANTS

In the desert, many plants have developed interesting ways to survive the arid conditions. In some areas, dew is the only water that will reach ground level for most of the year and some plants make use of this source, often storing the water in succulent leaves.

Other plants produce seeds that are able to survive long periods of drought and germinate only after sufficient rain. Some protect their seeds with older plant material and release them only after rain. Subsequently, these plants develop quickly. Their life cycles last only a few weeks and during this time they'll have to produce new seeds that will lie dormant until the next rain.

Some 80 per cent of all plant species in the UAE appear to be winter annuals, having adjusted to a life cycle that takes advantage of the winter rain. Some of the perennial plants also depend on the relatively reliable rainfall.

No one knew the plants' life cycles better than the nomadic Bedouin. For example, after the autumn rain or *wasmi*, they'd look for the desert truffle, *faqa'a*, that starts growing in the desert.

Sodom's apple.

Malaiha or southwards to Bidayar Al Ashkar – where there are high dunes overlooking vast open spaces with smaller dunes below. There are no specific routes to follow and you'll need to be an experienced sand-dune driver to get to either of these spots.

Driving on these high dunes is a true test of your driving skills and your vehicle's performance. Your tyre pressures should be approximately 15–18 Psi (depending on your 4x4's requirements) and you should be extra careful while negotiating any sudden drops.

Don't limit yourself to driving: leave your vehicle in a safe place and climb a dune to see the panoramic views.

Overnight camping

If you're interested in camping, take the road from Qarn Nazwa – where you should zero your odometer – and drive in a northeasterly direction towards the village of Nazwa. If you plan to stay near the road, turn left (at 3.8km/N25°01.731' E55°40.781') into a wooded area 200–300m from the road, where there's an ideal site for a large number of campers and numerous trees provide shade during the day. The flat, relatively hard ground makes this area ideal for pitching tents while the sand-dunes nearby are a great place for children to discover the desert flora and fauna of the UAE.

More seasoned campers should turn right (at 3km) and drive northwards to the high dunes a kilometre away. These are some of the highest in the area and the trees and depressions within the sand dunes are ideal for overnight desert camping.

The surrounding dunes make for a rewarding expedition. There are several camel farms that turn their animals loose to browse during the day. A visit to the old and new villages at Tawi Nazwa will give a further insight into UAE village life (N25°03.152' E55°41.695').

On an Emirates Holidays safari, you can combine the wildlife with the high life.

We know that great overland tours can really make a holiday. So we seek out some of the most exciting, most original experiences on offer. Fly-In safaris in Africa. Elephant trekking through dense jungles. Victoria Falls seen from a helicopter. It's the kind of attention to detail that makes Emirates Holidays' value unbeatable. So book now. Call your travel agent or Emirates Holidays on the number below.

Emirates Holidays

IT'S THE DETAILS THAT MAKE THE DIFFERENCE

ROUTE 2 NAZWA–FOSSIL ROCK

This enjoyable outing in the vicinity of Dubai and Sharjah can be covered in half a day. It could be combined with other trips to introduce you to the desert and its dunes before getting started on longer off-road adventures into the mountains.

In a number of places along the route there are several tracks from which to choose and distances could be slightly different from those recorded in the text.

How to get there

At Al Hibab Roundabout (N25°02.135' E55°35.486' – see previous chapter) zero your odometer, adjust your tyre pressures – you can do this later if you carry a tyre-pressure gauge – and stock up with fuel, water and food, then drive to the

IN BRIEF

STARTING POINT: Al Hibab Roundabout.
FINISHING POINT: Fossil Rock (Jebel Malaiha).
DISTANCE: 32km.
TIME REQUIRED: Half a day.
CATEGORY: 4x4 only.
HIGHLIGHTS: The village of Nazwa, red sand-dunes, desert vegetation, Wadi Al Faya, Jebel Al Faya, Camel Hump and Fossil Rock.

junction with the Nazwa road (8.3km).

The first two outcrops on either side of the highway (N24°59.925' E55°39.680') indicate you've reached this junction and a quick climb up either one is rewarding. Not only is there a 360-degree panoramic view of the surrounding flatland that will help you get your bearings, but there are also deposits of marine fossils.

At Nazwa Junction, turn left past the adjacent roundabout and head in a northeasterly direction on a tarmac road towards the village of Nazwa. If you're camping overnight, the area just before Nazwa is ideal, with small dunes and several patches of shady *ghaf* trees neatly cropped by the numerous camels in the area. This is also a good spot for birdwatching (12km/ (N25°01.781' E55°40.363').

Both Camel Hump (foreground) and Fossil Rock (background) boast marine fossils.

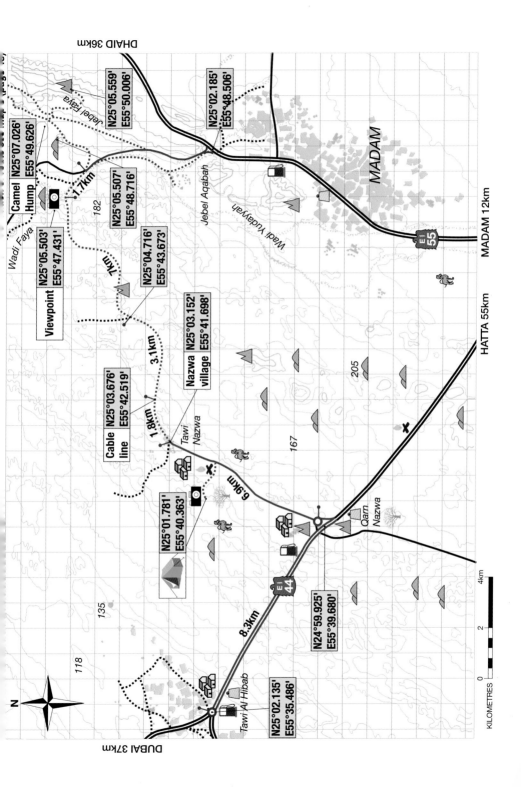

DHAID 36km

Camel **N25°07.026'**
Hump **E55°49.626'**

Jebel Faya

Wadi Faya

N25°05.559'
E55°50.006'

N25°02.185'
E55°48.506'

Viewpoint **N25°05.503'**
E55°47.431'

1.7km

182

N25°05.507'
E55°48.716'

7km

N25°04.716'
E55°43.673'

Jebel Aqabah

Wadi Yudayyah

MADAM

E1 55

MADAM 12km

3.1km

Nazwa **N25°03.152'**
village **E55°41.698'**

Cable **N25°03.676'**
line **E55°42.519'**

1.8km

Tawi Nazwa

205

HATTA 55km

167

6.9km

N25°01.781'
E55°40.363'

Qarn Nazwa

E1 44

N24°59.925'
E55°39.680'

135

118

N

8.3km

Tawi Al Hibab

N25°02.135'
E55°35.486'

DUBAI 37km

KILOMETRES 0   2   4km

A convoy of vehicles descends from the dunes into Wadi Al Faya.

The asphalt road ends at the village of Nazwa (15.2km/N25°03.152' E55°41.698'), where new houses have replaced the old huts found there just a few years ago. Numerous camels and cow and goat pens indicate a still-traditional way of life, making the drive through the village all the more interesting. Beyond Nazwa you'll drive past a farm into a dune area so, before you get stuck in the soft sand, reduce your tyre pressures to the recommended level of 15–18 Psi (depending on your 4x4's requirements), if you haven't already done so.

The desert

Leaving the village, turn right at a fork (15.4km/N25°03.244' E55°41.732') and drive towards a grove of *ghaf* trees. At 15km you'll reach more *ghaf* trees, farmland and animal pens – this is the site of the old village of Nazwa, which was still standing in 1986. Next, follow the track running along a cable line (17km/N25°03.676' E55°42.519') in a northeasterly direction to a flat gravel plain from where you can see Fossil Rock straight ahead of you and Jebel Faya to the right, before the track descends into a dip.

Continue following the cable lines until you reach a fork where the cable lines abruptly change direction (20.1km/N25°04.716' E55°43.673'). Take the right-hand track and move away from the cables in an easterly direction.

The track continues eastwards and, a kilometre beyond the fork, crosses a couple of rocky outcrops, almost levelled by sand and weathering in recent years (21km/N25°04.949' E55°44.060'). Some 3.4km beyond this point you'll reach a triple fork where you should take the central track across a gravel plain towards Jebel Faya (24.4km/N25°04.975' E55°46.027'). There are several tracks beyond the triple fork, which might seem a bit confusing, but at this stage you need to head in a northeasterly direction towards the left-hand edge of Jebel Faya.

You may have to drive up a few fairly steep dunes along this section, so increase your momentum before reaching them. At the edge of these dunes is one of the highlights of the trip: a look-out point from where you can look down on Wadi Al Faya with Fossil Rock and a high dune in the distance (27.1km/N25°05.503' E55°47.431').

CAMELS

Camels are the most frequently encountered animals in the desert, and desert dwellers were once dependent on them for their very survival. Camels were, in fact, the best friends of desert dwellers, who took almost as much care of them as they did of themselves, depending on them for their mobility, for transporting goods, for milk, meat and companionship. Even the coat of camels was used as wool for making rugs, clothing, tents and ropes, while leather from camels was used for containers to carry water and milk, and for drums.

Although the lifestyle of the population has changed drastically over recent decades, camels are still kept in great numbers, but for different reasons. Milk production is still significant, but the camel's most important role today is as a racing animal.

Camels are still traded in camel souks such as in Buraimi and other places in Oman, fetching from Dhs1,000 to Dhs5,000 a camel – they're sold for meat, milk, their hides or breeding purposes. Racing camels, however, go for much more, selling for between Dhs2,000 and Dhs20,000 an animal.

Camel races ensure the very survival of the camel today. Some oasis dwellers with prize camels keep them as studs and allow neighbouring camel farmers to breed their camels with them, but they still earn most of their money from the races themselves.

It's the female camels that are used for racing; they belong to the best bloodlines, and preferred breeds are the Shaheen and Hamloul. They're weaned from their mothers by the age of one and start racing at about two years, initially for races of only two to three kilometres. Later, they race for between eight to 16 kilometres, sometimes at speeds of up to 12 kilometres an hour – a true test of endurance. Racing camels have a specialised diet, being fed dates, fresh greens, barley, alfalfa and hay, with vitamin supplements.

As beasts of the desert, camels are superbly well equipped. They've been known to go without water for up to three weeks at a stretch, even in temperatures of 50°C. They're able to make various physiological adaptations to survive in the extreme conditions, such as adapting their body temperatures to the surrounding temperature so they don't lose precious water by sweating, and circulating water within their systems, so they don't need to urinate if they don't get enough water.

Their large feet facilitate easy movement over soft sand, while the fact that camels have three ankle joints – unlike other mammals, including humans, which have two – allows them to flex their feet more, making it easier to ascend or descend the slopes of dunes.

Camels are even conservation-conscious. They are browsers and nibble at foliage, then move on, instead of wastefully uprooting whole plants, as other animals such as sheep and goats do, and leaving an area devoid of vegetation. in additon, as they move around, their long eyelashes and bristles on their snouts help pollinate bushes and trees.

Camels also provide an important link with tradition. Because racing camels and good breeding stock fetch such high prices, it enables older members of the Arab population, who want to live near nature in the traditional manner, to do just that while raising their camels. Although you may see many camels wandering on the roadside (and even on the road!), there are no feral camels in the UAE – they all belong to someone.

Wadi Al Faya

Wadi Al Faya is one of the few remaining desert wadis that still carry flood waters from the Hajar Mountains into the desert before the water dissipates into the dunes near the Sharjah–Al Dhaid Road. This wadi probably stretched into the sea during heavy floods in the past. It's a comparatively lush area with many bends and is at its best after a flood, when a variety of plant species sprout forth.

Zero your odometer at the look out and, once you've driven down to the wadi, work your way towards the high dune, crossing the main track through the wadi (0.4km/N25°05.440' E55°47.693') and driving to another track that runs parallel to the main track 200m away (0.6km/N25°05.471' E55°47.804'). Turn right and follow this track until you reach a tar road a little more than a kilometre further on (1.7km/N25°05.120' E55°48.244'). Cross the tar and continue

Marine fossils typical of those found on Camel Hump and Fossil Rock.

towards the base of the main dune (2.9km/N25°05.507' E55°48.716'). The elevation at the base of the dune is 149m and its height is 225m.

Driving up this dune is quite difficult but a climb on foot to the top is rewarding. If you want to try driving up, approach it from the right-hand (Jebel Faya) side and work your way up to the top. If you're not confident in your dune-driving abilities you shouldn't venture on to this area because it's covered with soft sand where the tracks are neither fixed nor compacted.

On reaching the top of the dune, you should see a line of several rocky outcrops among the dunes leading to Fossil Rock 3km away. At one time these were probably part of the same range of mountains but they've since been separated by shifting sand.

Camel Hump

To get from the base of the dune to a photogenic rocky outcrop known as Camel Hump, follow the track to the right of the dune in a northeasterly direction. From this track you can see the quarry at the foot of Jebel Faya. The track reaches some pylons (at 5.9km/N25°06.617' E55°49.455'). Don't follow the track beneath these pylons but continue to some smaller power lines at the end of the range of mountains closest to you. From here follow the track to the left back into the dunes (6.4km/N25°06.831' E55°49.611').

The first outcrop you'll reach – a piece of rock weathered to resemble a camel with its head up – is Camel Hump (7.9km/N25°07.026' E55°49.627'). Immediately adjacent to this rock is a deep slope that's sometimes used by off-road drivers to test their vehicles, and at other times by sand skiers.

On weekdays there's less traffic in the area, making it and the shaded area below the rock an ideal picnic spot. After a break here, and if you want to test your dune-driving skills, you can work your way northwards through the dunes towards Fossil Rock, or you can return (along the previous track) to the main track and continue along it until you reach some pylons just before the village of Khatam (9.9km/N25°07.657' E55°50.311').

Below the pylons, take the track to the left and drive in a westerly direction back into the dunes. This track is compacted with gravel, making for easier driving. Drive 900m along the electrical pylons and turn north towards Fossil Rock (10.8km/N25°07.764' E55°49.807'). The drive from this point is classified as medium to difficult.

Fossil Rock (Jebel Malaiha)

Although there are several interesting outcrops before you reach Fossil Rock (Jebel Malaiha), the best part of this trip is still to come. Work your way right round a small outcrop to the right of Fossil Rock, then gather speed and take the track up towards the rock, just beneath its highest vertical face. Continue your climb until you reach a large boulder before the track turns down again. This is the highest point you can reach in a 4x4 and, even from here, the view is awesome (12.7km/N25°08.522' E55°49.991').

Leave your 4x4 here, taking the necessary precautions to prevent it from rolling down the steep hill. A climb up Fossil Rock can be quite an experience since there's an abundance of fossils and, if you find the right spot, you can see cross-sections of all kinds of marine life.

The hill is a geologist's and archaeologist's paradise and you may want to return and devote more time to exploring it. The views from the top over the plains are amazing and on a clear day Awir, Al Dhaid, Shawkah and even the Hajar Mountains can be seen. Many of the interesting rock formations provide shady places in which to relax.

Back in your 4x4, you can drive in a northerly direction for another 500 metres and then east, up towards the neck of Fossil Rock (N25°08.632' E55°50.096') and take the steep track down towards Malaiha. However, it should be noted that this route is both difficult and dangerous and therefore not a readily recommended one.

Rather turn southwards at Fossil Rock and take the track running eastwards towards Malaiha and Al Dhaid–Madam Highway. The track continues through the farmlands of Malaiha (16.2km/N25°08.812' E55°51.740') and runs towards the highway. It reaches a roundabout (at 19.2km/N25°08.121' E55°52.974') and, immediately afterwards, a petrol station that can cater for your needs, including air for your tyres if necessary. Travelling north along this highway will take you to Al Dhaid and south to the Madam Roundabout.

The drive up Fossil Rock is fairly difficult but the view is magnificent.

ROUTE 3 WADI AND JEBEL AL FAYA

Wadi and Jebel ('Jebel' means 'mountain') Al Faya are on the western edge of the Madam Plains. Wadi Al Faya carries whatever is left of the rainwaters from the Hajar Mountains once it has passed through the Madam Plains. The wadi dissipates into the desert sand beyond Rashidiya, in the emirate of Sharjah, just before reaching the Sharjah–Al Dhaid Highway.

This wide, quiet wadi winds through the desert in a northerly and northwesterly direction. Because of its distance from the mountains and its porous characteristics, it takes a great deal of rain to get the water flowing in the

IN BRIEF

STARTING POINT: Rashidiya Interchange (ie Interchange 9) on the Sharjah–Al Dhaid Highway.
FINISHING POINT: Madam–Al Dhaid Road or Sharjah–Al Dhaid Highway Interchange (ie Interchange 11).
DISTANCE: 63km.
TIME REQUIRED: Half a day to one day.
CATEGORY: Sand and wadi driving – 4x4 only.
HIGHLIGHTS: A unique wadi winding through a rich desert landscape. Rashidiya, Muhafiz, Qarn Al Murra, Jebel Al Faya and Jebel Malaiha (Fossil Rock). The Sharjah Natural History Museum and Arabian Wildlife Centre are situated along this route.

wadi bed. Heavy rains in 1988 and 1990 produced flash floods of immense size that were carried long distances through the wadi, eventually creating lakes around Sayh Musannad, just before the Sharjah–Al Dhaid Road.

It's after such rains that the wadi and its elements are at their best and the majestic size of the wadi is realised. It turns green and blooms with desert plants, shrubs and flowers. The abundance of vegetation makes the trip through Wadi Al Faya a memorable one.

Getting there
There are several ways to get to Wadi Al Faya, including the following: from the Dubai–Hatta Road

Exploring the quarry near Tawi Salman – along the final section of the route.

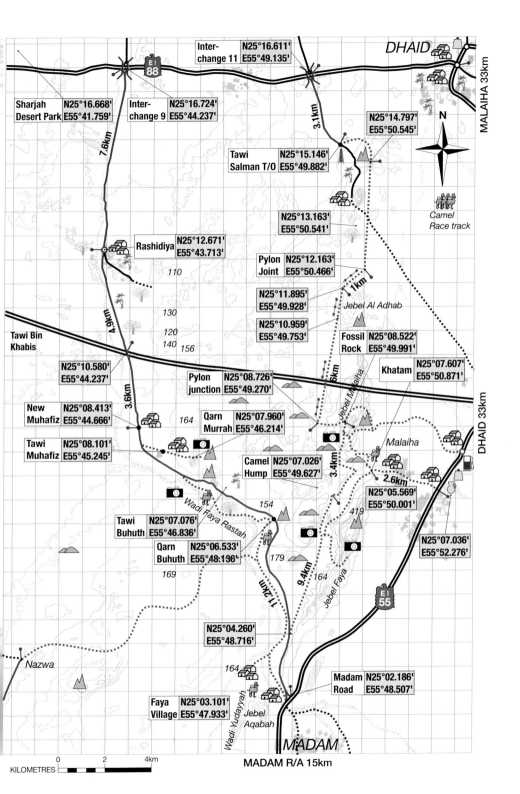

The track through Wadi Al Faya is compact and easy to drive on.

and through Nazwa (see previous chapter), via the Al Dhaid–Madam Road and via the Sharjah–Al Dhaid Road. The latter approach is recommended because it's the simplest to follow.

The starting point for this route is the Rashidiya Interchange (ie Interchange 9) on the Sharjah–Al Dhaid Highway. The interchange is approximately 32 kilometres from the Book Roundabout (also known as Cultural Square) in Sharjah.

There are three notable attractions *en route* to this junction: the Discovery Centre (for children of the age of 13 or older), Sharjah Natural History Museum and Arabian Wildlife Centre, the latter two being part of Sharjah Desert Park. Since a visit could take at least two to three hours, it would perhaps be better to leave these educational centres for the return journey, when you'll benefit from

experiencing nature in its own setting.

Zero your odometer as you turn off the Al Dhaid Road at Interchange 9 (N25°16.724' E55°44.237') and drive on the tar road south towards Rashidiya. It's probable that this new road was built directly on the track that previously ran through Wadi Al Faya. The road is straight and passes through a gravel plain dotted with shrubs, notably Sodom's Apple. This plant, which has an attractive, waxy flower, is abundant throughout this route and is an indication of the wadi-type characteristics of the surrounding land.

Rashidiya and beyond

The single carriageway south reaches a roundabout at the small village of Rashidiya (at 7.6km/N25°12.671' E55°43.713'), where there are a few houses, farms, animal pens, several date-palm plantations and numerous *ghaf* – the indigenous tree of the area. A drive through the village gives an idea of contemporary UAE village life.

Wadi Al Faya is at its widest here; northwest of the village it merges with the sand and disappears.

Continue south beyond Rashidiya towards the new and old villages of Muhafiz, crossing the road running northwest (which takes you to Tawi Bin Khabis and the Dubai–Awir Road) *en route* (12.5km/N25°10.580' E55°44.237'). Next up are the new village of Muhafiz (15.6km/N25°08.413' E55°44.666') and, after a left turn (at 16.1km/N25°08.188' E55°44.814'), the old village, Tawi Muhafiz, populated by members of the Bani Qitab tribe.

Qarn Murrah

Beyond Muhafiz head eastwards towards Qarn Murrah, the closest rocky outcrop. Although there are no fixed tracks, the sand is quite compact, and you should be

The car loan with the lowest interest rates in town!

DRIVE

- Up to 60 months repayment period
- Zero down payment option
- Insurance at competitive rates
- Fast and friendly processing
- And more

Only meBANK offers so many services, 24 hours a day, seven days a week.

BANK
More bank for my money

For more, call 800 4644.
www.emiratesbank.com/mebank

" I planned to buy a V6.
The bank got me a V8.

able to reach the top of the hill (20km/ N25°07.960' E55°46.214') with no trouble. The rocky peak consists of a number of interesting shapes and forms, mostly bright brown or pink in colour. A short climb to the peak will reward you with a 360-degree panoramic view, while there are interesting drives of varying degrees of difficulty on all sides of the hill.

After the scenic visit to Qarn Murrah return to the village and take the tarmac road in a southeasterly direction back to Tawi Muhafiz where you should again zero your vehicle's odometer.

From here you can – if you're in a hurry – continue on the tarmac road along Wadi Al Faya in a southwesterly direction. On the way you'll pass the village of Tawi Buhuth (2.4km/N25°07.076' E55°46.836'). The road runs close to Jebel Al Faya and along Wadi Al Faya until it finally reaches the Al Dhaid–Madam Road (11.2km/ N25°02.186' E55°48.507') just beyond Faya village.

Alternatively, if you're interested in more off-road driving, you should depart the tarmac road near Tawi Muhafiz and explore Wadi Al Faya. Heading towards the Al Dhaid–Madam Road, simply keep the new highway on your left.

Wadi Al Faya

The sandy wadi is fairly compact for the most part, except after flooding when you'll find puddles of water, mud, tree trunks and branches stuck to the uprooted plants. Often you'll also find camels crossing the wadi in a straight line.

There's an abundance of desert vegetation, and the reptiles and insects make Wadi Al Faya a worthwhile trip. From parasitic plants and desert bushes to colourful birds, you can see them all while travelling through here.

To catch a glimpse of the smaller reptiles and flowering plants, try stopping under one of the *ghaf* trees, where you're sure to encounter some of these tiny yet hardy inhabitants.

If you've made it this far, there's no

The slopes surrounding Qarn Murrah provide routes of varying degrees of difficulty.

possibility of getting lost, since the well-defined wadi with sandy edges leads you through and over a sandy track towards your destination. The red colour of the winding sandy embankments, decorated with colourful plants, enhances the panoramic view after practically every bend in the wadi.

One of the plants growing in abundance in Wadi Al Faya is *ashur*, the Sodom's Apple mentioned earlier. It's a large shrub which bears waxy white-and-pink flowers. Although the Bedouin make charcoal from its stem and use the white resin as a laxative, animals do not like to eat it. You'll see many of these shrubs on the last 10 kilometres of this wadi bed.

Two highlights of this short drive are several pleasant camping spots shaded by *ghaf* trees (particularly at N25°06.688' E55°47.186') and an interesting outcrop of rocks (N25°06.533' E55°48.136').

As you reach the end of the wadi it widens again and the Madam–Al Dhaid Road can be spotted immediately above it. You are now at the end of the first section of this route.

SHARJAH DESERT PARK

You'll find the Sharjah Desert Park 28km from the centre of Sharjah, *en route* to Al Dhaid. It has three components spread over one square kilometre: the Natural History Museum, Arabian Wildlife Centre and the Children's Farm.

The museum provides people of all ages with an opportunity to learn about the flora and fauna of the Arabian Desert and has five main exhibition halls: A Journey through Sharjah, Man and the Environment, A Journey through Time, The Living Desert and The Living Sea.

The Arabian Wildlife Centre showcases the rich diversity of fauna in the Arabian Peninsula as well as teaching about species which have become, and are becoming, extinct. It contains more than 100 species of animals, and is divided into a reptile and insect house, aviary, nocturnal houses, viewing area and a section for large predators and monkeys. The children's farm gives children a chance to come into close contact with farm animals, such as donkeys, goats, sheep and chickens.

The Breeding Centre for Endangered Arabian Wildlife is also located near the museum. It aims to breed the indigenous animals of Arabia which are under threat of extinction, to reintroduce them into their natural habitat and also to provide zoos with some of the indigenous animals of the area.

The desert park makes for an enjoyable day's outing and is open every day except Monday. For enquiries call (06) 531 1999.

Trip through Jebel Al Faya

To continue exploring the wadi and Jebel
Al Faya, drive back 4km (N25°04.276'
E55°48.532') to the point where the road
runs close to Jebel Al Faya and along
Wadi Al Faya. Turn 90 degrees right and
drive 300m away from the tarmac on to
the track running east (N25°04.260'
E55°48.716'). Then continue in a
northerly direction parallel to the pylons
running along the foothills of Jebel Al
Faya. This track joins another track
running into an opening in the mountain
(8.4km/ N25°06.367' E55°49.520'), used
by local quarry companies.

On Fridays and holidays the quarry is
inactive, giving rock climbers an
opportunity to practice their skills on its
sheer walls. Jebel Al Faya is also
geologically interesting in that various
types of fossils are found there. Using the
quarry track to the top of Jebel Al Faya is
very dusty but exhilarating. The view from
the plateau on the summit is 360-degree
panoramic as far as the eye can see.

Driving north from Jebel Al Faya will
take you to the old village of Khatam
(11.9km/N25°07.607' E55°50.871'),
situated on the outskirts of Malaiha.

To reach the Al Dhaid–Madam Road
continue on the track running directly east
for another 2.6km. An archaeological site
400 metres south of this point N25°07.036'
E55°52.276'), right off the Al Dhaid–
Madam Road, is worth exploring.

An archaeological site near the village of Malaiha on Al Dhaid–Madam Road.

The quarry track to the top of Jebel Al Faya is dusty but exhilarating.

Fossil Rock

To get to Fossil Rock from the new village of Khatam (next to the old village), head in a northwesterly direction, working your way slowly up the dunes while keeping Fossil Rock in sight.

After reaching Fossil Rock (N25°08.522' E55°49.991') and spending time there, zero your odometer and drive east towards the electrical pylons running in a north–south direction.

Drive north after reaching the pylons (1.4km/N25°08.726' E55°49.270'), on the compacted track running alongside them. Where the track is partially covered by dunes, slow down and cross the sand carefully. The area is undisturbed and wild and makes you feel far from any civilisation. This track is not travelled often and could become completely buried beneath shifting sand in a few years' time.

The track continues north in a straight line after passing Jebel Al Adhab (6.8km/N25°10.959' E55°49.753').

Turning in a northeasterly direction (at 7.9km/N25°11.895' E55°49.928'), the pylons join another set (at 8.9km/ N25°12.163' E55°50.466') and head north again.

The view of rolling sand-dunes is beautiful along this section and there's a pleasant picnic spot (at 10.8km/ N25°13.163' E55°50.541') where clusters of *ghaf* trees on the high dunes beckon.

The track continues north to a quarry and a beautiful rock formation with a beautifully weathered wall in the form of diagonal layers (14.2 km/N25°14.797' E55°50.545'). Tawi Salman, where a large building stands incongruously in the distance, is reached after another kilometre. Turn left here and take the tarmac road leading to Interchange 11 on the Sharjah–Al Dhaid Road (20.2km/ N25°16.611' E55°49.135').

Travel in a westerly direction along this road and stop to explore the Sharjah Natural History Museum and Arabia's Wildlife Centre on the way back.

ROUTE 4 WADI AL QAWR

As one of the oldest caravan routes from the Arabian Gulf to the Gulf of Oman, this route offers many fascinating spots for travellers interested in the UAE's cultural heritage, scenic beauty, lush oases and rustic architecture. Sitting with the old folk of the area and listening to their tales and reminiscences of adventurous trips along this once-flourishing route will make you eager to visit the wadi.

Some 50 years ago the coast-to-coast trip, which now takes only a few hours, would take several days in Land Rovers or Bedford trucks (see Ronald Codrai's introduction). The route lost its importance when the new tarmac road was built to carry traffic through Hatta to the Batinah Coast and on to Muscat.

There are two approaches from Madam

IN BRIEF

STARTING POINT: Madam Roundabout.
FINISHING POINT: Hatta.
DISTANCE: 80km one way.
TIME REQUIRED: One day but this route is also suitable for overnight camping.
CATEGORY: 4x4.
HIGHLIGHTS: Madam Plain, Jebel Rawdah, Al Qawr Oasis and village, old villages on the way to Aswad and various watch-towers and forts along the route.

Roundabout to this route: via Tawi Fili (recommended) or via Jebel Rawdah.

The route via Tawi Fili

To travel via Tawi Fili, zero your odometer at Madam Roundabout (N24°54.866' E55°46.638'), then drive north towards Al Dhaid. There are a couple of petrol stations along the way where you should fill up your tank because there aren't many others further on. There are also plenty of shops where you can buy food and drink. At the next roundabout (12.8km/N25°00.876' E55°48.363'), take the tarmac road that heads eastwards through many farmlands until it terminates at Tawi Fili (25.8km/N24°59.906' E55°55.915').

There's an old watch-tower 300m before the end of the tarmac road on the left-hand side that, together with a small fort at the end, highlights the fact that this was

A view of the entrance to Wadi Al Qawr from Jebel Rawdah.

once an important thoroughfare. The small buildings across the road from the fort must once have provided weary travellers with refreshments and accommodation and you can, in fact, still see a number of old bottle tops outside one of them.

From Tawi Fili several tracks set off in a southerly direction. Pick the most prominent one and drive due south towards the most conspicuous peak, Jebel Rawdah. There will also be another range of mountains flanking your left.

Continuing towards Jebel Rawdah, the next landmark is the cone-shaped Qarn Al Himar (meaning 'Outcrop of the Donkey') (34.2km/N24°55.459' E55°57.015'). Beyond Qarn Al Himar, the jagged foothills on the left and the mountains on the right close in on the track (35.6km/N24°54.850' E55°57.360'). (Jebel Rawdah is the first mountain you'll see when you're driving from Dubai towards Hatta. It's one of the highest and closest mountain ranges to Dubai, peaking at 770 metres above sea level.)

The whole area is very rich in fossils and a variety of geologically-interesting rocks and patches of plantations are visible near the foothills. The western portion of the mountain has a crescent shape and resembles the crater of a volcano. There are myriad colours, ranging from white, beige and light green to dark, almost black-brown, in the rocks. The peak is easily accessible because of its proximity to the main road and gradual ascent.

At 3.4km beyond Qarn Al Himar the road forks at the spot where the alternative approach route via Jebel Rawdah joins this route (39km/ N24°53.804' E55°57.883'). Zero your odometer here.

The route via Jebel Rawdah

Arriving at Madam Roundabout from Al Ain, Dubai or Al Dhaid, drive in an easterly direction on the tarmac road

A group of children inspecting the interior of the old watch-tower at Tawi Fili.

towards Hatta. After 4km you'll enter Oman and, some 5km further, you'll pass some government buildings and a mosque on your left, while the foothills you can see behind them are those of Jebel Rawdah. Immediately after the sign 'Al-Barwani Crushers', turn left off the highway onto a tarmac road (10.9km/ N24°53.338' E55°52.682') and right at the fork immediately after that.

Continue along this tarmac road until you reach another fork (12.6km/ N24°53.694' E55°53.651') and take the left-hand fork onto a gravel track that

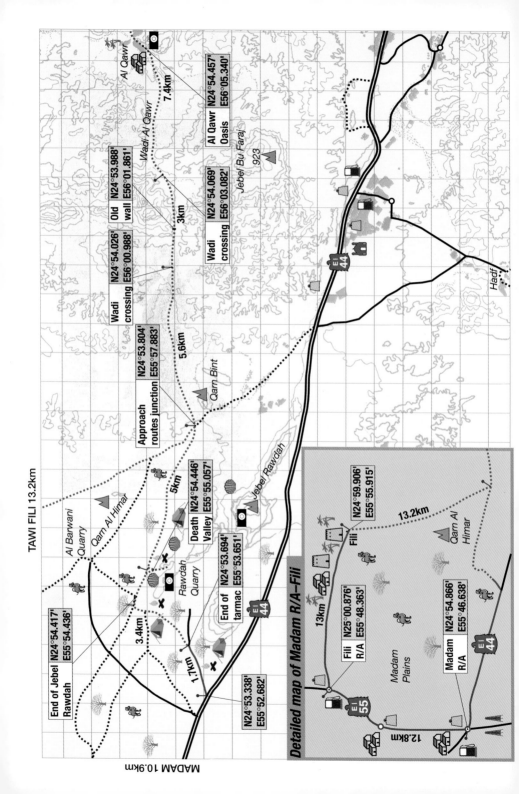

TAWI FILI 13.2km

MADAM 10.9km

End of Jebel Rawdah N24°54.417' E55°54.436'

Al Barwani Quarry

Qarn Al Himar

5km

3.4km

1.7km

N24°53.338' E55°52.682'

Rawdah Quarry

Death Valley N24°54.446' E55°55.057'

End of tarmac N24°53.694' E55°53.651'

E1 44

Jebel Rawdah

Approach routes junction N24°53.804' E55°57.883'

Qarn Bint

5.6km

Wadi crossing N24°54.026' E56°00.988'

Old wall N24°53.988' E56°01.861'

3km

Wadi crossing N24°54.069' E56°03.082'

Jebel Bu Faraj 923

Al Qawr Oasis N24°54.457' E56°05.340'

N24°53.988' E56°01.861'

7.4km

Al Qawr

Wadi Al Qawr

E1 44

Hadf

Detailed map of Madam R/A–Fili

N24°59.906' E55°55.915'

Fili

13km

Fili R/A N25°00.876' E55°48.363'

E1 55

Madam Plains

13.2km

Qarn Al Himar

Madam R/A N24°54.866' E55°46.638'

E1 44

12.8km

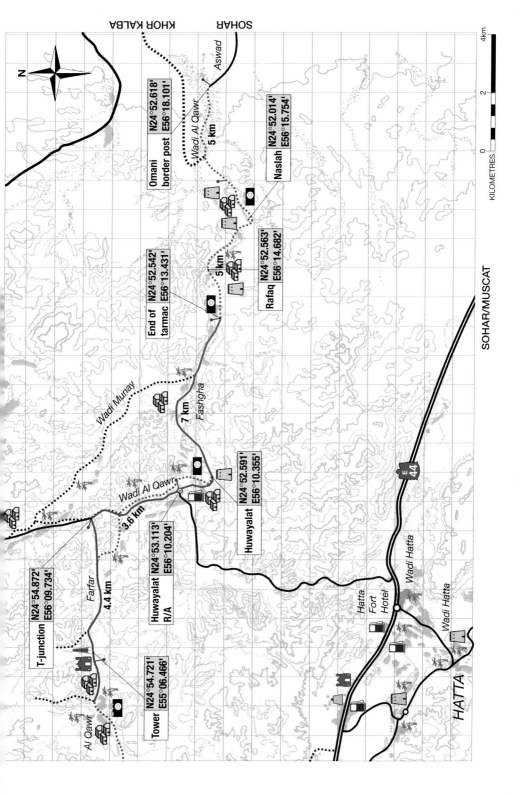

skirts the base of some gravel hills. After 700m these gravel hills veer away from the track as the route continues in the same direction (northeastwards). At this point you can see Rawdah Quarry in a valley some distance to your right (while, if you'd taken the left-hand fork immediately after turning off the Dubai–Hatta Highway, you'd have travelled to Al-Barwani Crushers Quarry).

After a further 200m, take the fork to the right (13.5km) and travel alongside the fence of a farm, turning towards the beginning of Jebel Rawdah beyond the farm.

Continue along the base of Jebel Rawdah until you reach the entrance to a small wadi that cuts into the mountain (16km/N24°54.446' E55°55.057'). During the past 20 years or so there have always

been a number of dead camels in various degrees of decomposition in this area, leading the writer to name this small wadi Death Valley. Perhaps Mystery Valley would have been a more appropriate name because of the mystery as to why these camels come to this spot to die. . . .

You can drive 300m up this wadi before exploring it further on foot. In fact, should you wish to explore the Jebel Rawdah area, there are several tracks leading into small, flat gravel wadis close to the mountain. The pleasant camping spots have made this area popular with local families and there are more secluded sites further up the mountain. The variations of colour here (black indicates a presence of iron ore), the flora and fauna and the rocks themselves all have a

Jebel Rawdah is a fascinating mountain for the whole family to explore.

magical effect on outdoor enthusiasts.

And, should you decide to climb the mountain, the huge overhanging boulders create shady resting spots. It's an exhilarating trip to the top and from three-quarters of the way up you have a beautiful view down into the wadis and plains below. A short climb to the flat ridge leaves you with an easy climb to the peak.

After exiting Death Valley (16.7km/ N24°54.445' E55°55.059'), continue eastwards towards Wadi Al Qwar. There are several tracks from which to choose, most of which gradually move away from the mountain towards the point where this approach route joins the approach route from Tawi Fili, just 5km from Death Valley (21.7km/N24°53.804' E55°57.883'). Zero your odometer here. Along the final section of this approach route you'll probably notice more camel carcasses and bones.

The combined route into Wadi Al Qawr

Beyond the junction of the two approach routes, take the left track proceeding in an easterly direction into Wadi Al Qawr. There are two interesting wadi-crossings that provide splendid opportunities for laid-back picnicking and exploring – especially during a wet season (at 5.6km and 8.6km).

A major landmark between these two crossings is an old stone wall that at one time may have shepherded travellers through some sort of checkpoint (N24°53.988' E56°01.861'). There's another wadi crossing at the old village of Al Qawr where, sadly, a dying oasis tells a story of more prosperous days.

Beyond the old village the track changes to a tar road and passes the new village with its white-painted houses, modern telecommunications tower (N24°54.721' E55°06.466') and a conspicious mosque (16km).

This old fort overlooks Wadi Al Qawr and the village of Al Naslah.

This section ends at a T-junction (20.4km/N24°54.872' E56°09.734') where there's a telephone booth. Turn right (southeastwards) here and travel along the tarmac road south to Huwaylat and a roundabout (24km/N24°53.113' E56°10.204').

The roundabout is bordered by several shops where you can once again stock up with food and drink. From the roundabout take the tarmac road past the village of Huwaylat.

Huwaylat

Huwaylat (25.1km/N24°52.591' E56°10.355') is an old oasis cum-trading-post-cum-rest-stop for people travelling to the Omani Coast; the remains of an old mosque and *falaj* here remind visitors of its heyday.

There was also a rest-house that provided not only food and shelter for travellers of yesteryear but also vital supplies of petrol. Weary travellers arriving in the late afternoon would have waited in the village until the next morning for the border post at Aswad to reopen. Huwaylat, with its old and new terraced gardens lining the wadi, has now become a resort and second home for rich city dwellers. A drive through the new village gives visitors a chance to catch a glimpse of modern village life in the UAE.

Continuing eastwards into Wadi Al Qawr, you have the opportunity to see old dwellings juxtaposed with newly-constructed houses. The *aflaj* most often flow parallel to the wadi, carrying water to the oases. Most of the year there's also water flowing in the wadi itself. Some of the villages lined up one after the other along the route to Aswad are Fashgha, Rafaq and Al Naslah.

The tarmac ends in Wadi Al Qawr (31km/N24°52.542' E56°13.431') shortly after the road passes Rafaq, where an old watch-tower overlooks the village and wadi (33.2km/N24°52.563' E56°14.682'). Not far from Rafaq (at 36km/N24°52.014' E56°15.754') is an old fort, strategically situated on a hill overlooking the wadi and the village of Al Naslah. The remains of an old mosque are situated close to the fort; the ruins are worth exploring and make excellent photographic subjects. In addition to the fort, Al Naslah boasts a second fortification, a watch-tower.

From this point, driving in a northeasterly to easterly direction, you'll soon reach the Omani border post at Aswad (41km/N24°52.618' E56°18.101'). Here, at the end of the route, the wadi terminates in a fan-shaped gravel plain.

There are two easy ways to return home from here. The first is to return to Hatta through Huwaylat. However, if your destination is Khor Kalba or Fujairah, take the track 2.5km (N24°52.639' E56°16.739') before the Aswad border post. This track runs north along the border with Oman and eventually ends up at these centres.

FRUIT OF THE DESERT

While researching this book on the plains below Jebel Rawdah, after January rains, the writer spotted a group of young nationals in two Land Rovers. They would get into their vehicles and drive a couple of kilometres, jump out, examine a bush and extract something which they ate.

It turned out that they were after a parasitic plant known as *daghabis*, shaped very much like asparagus spears. The edible portion is the thin tip on top, which has a sweet taste. It grows in the middle of the bush and is protected and shaded in this environment. The boys mentioned *daghabis* grows only after the rains and is very tasty and nutritious. They had learned about it

from their grandfathers and other elders in their families. The bush it grows on is called *kharman*.

It's refreshing to know there's an insurance policy that keeps you on the road

ROUTE 5 HADF

South of Mudayrah, Hadf village is situated in a lush green valley surrounded by mountains. Besides the picturesque surroundings and the natural setting, Wadi Hadf offers an enjoyable drive. The route incorporates a section of the wadi, some lovely viewpoints and a mountain pass with a panorama of layers of mountains in the distance – each one a different colour.

This is an easy drive for a newcomer to the UAE or 4x4 driving as it's not too long, not too difficult and not too far from the Dubai–Hatta Highway.

How to get there
The route starts 5km west of Mudayrah on the main Dubai–Hatta Highway.

IN BRIEF

STARTING POINT: The Dubai–Hatta Road.
FINISHING POINT: Mudayrah.
DISTANCE: 18-km round trip from the Dubai–Hatta Road.
TIME REQUIRED: Half a day or less from Dubai or Hatta. May also be combined with other routes in the area.
CATEGORY: With the exception of the wadi and the last section (a rough mountain pass), the route can be negotiated in a normal saloon car.
HIGHLIGHTS: The gorge, old village and oasis of Hadf, as well as the ruins of ancient houses above the wadi.

This is 24km from the Madam Roundabout if you're travelling from Dubai towards Hatta and 15km from the Hatta Fort Hotel Roundabout if you're travelling from Hatta.

Zero your odometer at the turn-off leading south to Hadf (N24°51.294' E55°59.906') and you'll soon reach the new village of Hadf (5.7km/N24°48.789' E56°01.513').

You may want to explore the new village and try chatting to some of the interesting old residents who gather round the mosque after praying. A knowledge of Arabic would be helpful but don't let a lack of this deter you. The old village of Hadf, also known as Sinadil, is situated a kilometre

The Hadf route offers an enjoyable drive, close to the main Dubai–Hatta Road.

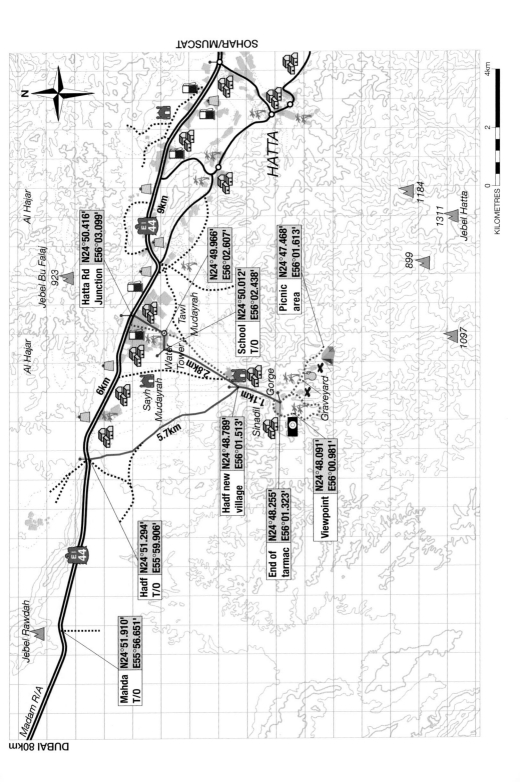

SOHAR/MUSCAT

DUBAI 80km

Madam R/A

Jebel Rawdah

N

Al Hajar

Jebel Bu Falaj
923

Al Hajar

HATTA

Jebel Hatta
1311
1184
899
1097

E 44

E 44

9km

6km

5.7km

2.8km

1.1km

Sayh Mudayrah

Water Tower

Tawi Mudayrah

Sinadil Gorge

Graveyard

Mahda T/O N24°51.910' E55°55.906'

Hadf T/O N24°51.294' E55°59.906'

Hatta Rd Junction N24°50.416' E56°03.099'

N24°49.966' E56°02.607'

School T/O N24°50.012' E56°02.438'

Picnic area N24°47.468' E56°01.613'

Hadf new village N24°48.789' E56°01.513'

End of tarmac N24°48.255' E56°01.323'

Viewpoint N24°48.091' E56°00.981'

KILOMETRES
0   2   4km

An old graveyard, typical of those in the UAE, is situated close to Wadi Hadf.

south of the new village and marks the end of the tarmac road and the beginning of the main part of the trip (6.8km/N24°48.255' E56°01.323').

The gorge

A gorge is visible from the old village. It's 15–20m deep, beautifully formed and carved by the flow of water over the centuries. To enter the gorge, you'll have to go further down the wadi and approach it on foot, but you can also walk along the top and enjoy the interesting view en route.

The 300-m course of the gorge has water running through it almost all year round. From here you can see the peaks of Hatta Mountains, rising more than 1,000m on your left.

The track to the wadi becomes narrow and divides a kilometre away from the old village. Keep right here (the left-hand-track proceeds along the side of the wadi) and after a further 180m there's another

Looking into the deep, steep-sided gorge near the old village of Hadf.

fork. Take the left-hand track and you'll notice an old graveyard immediately to your right. The number of headstones is a sure sign that there once must have been a thriving settlement here.

You can drive up the wadi for about 1.4km, following a rocky and very narrow track that should not be attempted by the inexperienced. The vegetation in the oasis to the left of the wadi includes palm trees, citrus, mangoes and a mixture of vegetables, while the long bamboo shoots in the wadi are indicative of an abundance of water under the wadi bed. Above the wadi, on the right-hand side, are the ruins of more stone houses.

It's been said that some of these ruins are more than 1,000 years old and there's also a mosque with a low, two-foot wall where you can see the remains of the Mehrab (altar), indicating the direction in which to pray. Steps are curved into the mountainside showing a rough route from the top into the wadi.

This area is a dividing point in the Hajar Mountain Range. Some of the water flows towards the Oman coast and the rest to the Gulf. This may be the reason why it's such a lush and lovely spot. It takes about two hours to survey the whole scene but you could easily enjoy more time here, including a picnic (8.7km/N24°47.468' E56°01.613').

The mountain pass

Returning from the wadi you should explore the oasis, which is on the right-hand side coming from the old village (10.3km/N24°47.732' E56°00.960'). Follow the track past a fenced farm and then up the mountain to a viewpoint near the top. From here there's a stunning view of the area you've just explored to the south, with a backdrop of layers of mountain peaks (12.5km/N24°48.091' E56°00.981').

At the time of writing (2002), the section of the pass going down towards the old village was worse than the ascent. Back on the level plain, this track loops around the old village before bringing you back to the beginning of the asphalt road (14.1km/N24°48.464' E56°01.301') and

The ruins of the old village of Hadf are a kilometre south of the new village.

the new village of Hadf. From here you can return to the Dubai–Hatta Road through the village of Mudayrah.

Mudayrah

Mudayrah, which falls within the emirate of Ajman, is located just south of the Dubai–Hatta Road. It's a large, comparatively green

Wadi Hadf is rocky and narrow and should not be attempted by the inexperienced.

BIRD-WATCHING IN THE DESERT

The bird life in the UAE is surprisingly rich and diverse with more than 400 species recorded. The reason for this abundance is the UAE's location on an important migratory crossroads, where at least 320 migrants from Siberia and Central Asia have been identified. Some of these birds migrate through the country during spring and autumn, others overwinter during the cooler months.

This, however, does not mean there's a lack of colourful indigenous species to be seen and serious birdwatchers will always be on the look out for specials such as Chestnut-bellied Sandgrouse, White-collared Kingfisher, Hume's Wheatear and Purple Sunbird.

Birds tend to favour certain habitats and the species you're most likely to come across are those that thrive in the dunes, plains and mountains, with the wadis, villages and oases providing additional variety.

Few species of birds choose to live in the harsh desert with its limited food reserves. Of those that do, the most common are the larks and, of these, the Hoopoe Lark, which is well adapted to running through desert sands, is probably the most common resident. Another common smaller desert-breeding bird is the Black-crowned Finch Lark, known locally as the BCFL. Some other interesting species to watch out for include the Eagle Owl, Brown-necked Raven, Cream-coloured Courser, Stone Curlew and various species of sandgrouse.

In an interesting and unusual desert adaptation, the sandgrouse supply their young with water that they transport over large distances in their specially modified breast and belly feathers.

Among the species that prefer the rocky environment of the mountains, with their deeply-incised wadis, are the Egyptian and Griffon vultures, Kestrel, Little Owl, Desert Lark, Chukar and See-see partridges, Yellow-vented Bulbul, Arabian Babbler, Grey Wagtail, Yellow-throated Sparrow, Little Green Bee-eater, Pale Crag Martin, Blue Rock Thrush and several species of wheatear.

Newcomers to the region will benefit from a good guide to enhance their bird-watching activities and an ideal introduction to the birds of the UAE is *Birds of the Southern Gulf* by Dave Robinson and Adrian Chapman, published by Motivate.

---

village that fans out into an alluvial plain rich in soil, minerals and water. The water that flows down from the Hajar Mountains and Wadi Hadf into the plain was the reason for the region's development.

Mudayrah has grown into a sizeable village. People are tempted to settle here because, in addition to its fertile land and abundant water supply, it's conveniently located alongside a major highway.

There's ample greenery all round and the new houses, school and mosque, with their colourful doors, manage to preserve the traditional look of the area. The village has all the modern amenities with easy access to Hatta and Dubai. Mudayrah is 30km from Madam Roundabout and 9km from the Hatta Fort Hotel Roundabout.

Once you've driven through the village, you'll reach a school at a T-junction. At the school, turn right and proceed to a round-about 300m away (at 18km/N24°49.966' E56°02.607') and the highway is a short distance from it. There are two petrol stations near the junction and a number of shops selling food, pottery and other items.

ROUTE 6 HATTA POOLS

Hatta Pools, with their colorful rock faces and cascading waterfalls, are a picturesque destination with swimming opportunities in natural pools a welcome bonus.

This is an easily arranged trip that can be undertaken in half a day. The drive from Dubai to Hatta takes about an hour and is as fascinating as the destination itself, with the superb highway cutting through rolling dunes and mountain landscapes. The Hatta Fort Hotel is a popular mountain-resort complex and a drive to Hatta Pools could be followed by lunch at the hotel and a leisurely afternoon at its swimming pool – or you could even overnight there.

IN BRIEF

STARTING POINT: Hatta Fort Hotel Roundabout.
FINISHING POINT: Hatta Pools.
DISTANCE: 19km (one way).
TIME REQUIRED: Half a day or longer if preferred.
CATEGORY: The drive may be undertaken in a normal saloon car, although the last 500m may then have to be done on foot.
HIGHLIGHTS: Colorful mountain ranges, oases, a *falaj*, natural pools, waterfalls and the old village of Hatta.

How to get there

At the Hatta Fort Hotel Roundabout, which marks the end of the highway from Dubai to Hatta (N24°49.124' E56°08.056'), zero your odometer and, still on tarmac, turn right in a southwesterly direction towards Hatta village. You'll see the Hajar Mountains in front of you. After a short distance on this road continue straight, past a turn-off to the Hatta Heritage Village (2.5km/ N24°48.052' E56°07.025'). Soon you'll reach a small roundabout with a police station on one side and a power station on the other (2.6km/ N24°47.960' E56°06.886'). Turn south, past the new village and continue along the main road towards the mountains.

Hatta Heritage Village depicts the architecture of an ancient fortress village.

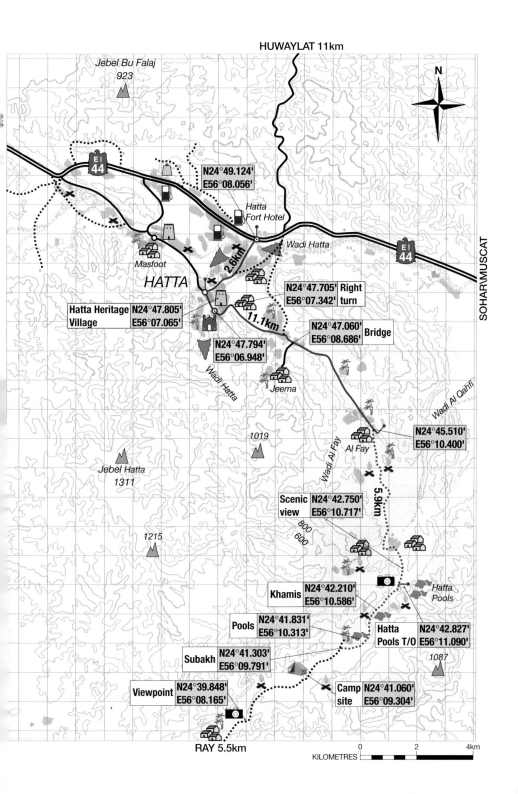

Hatta Heritage Village

If you're interested in a short side trip, and would like to learn a little about the history of Hatta, you can visit the Heritage Village.

The old village, recently renovated by the Dubai Government, has been turned into a tourist complex showcasing the traditional lifestyle of Hatta and its inhabitants. Depicting the ways of life of the past, models wearing traditional clothing of the region carry out their daily routine. Both the newly renovated Wali house, and the hamlet on the hill overlooking the oasis, provide further insight into the history of the ancient fortress village and are fine examples of village architecture of 400 years ago.

Beyond the roundabout, the main road

The village of Hatta is attractively set in a valley in the Hajar Mountains.

forks at a mosque (3.1km/N24°47.794' E56°06.948'). Keep right here and continue to a second fork at the school, where you go left (3.2km). Note the watch-tower on your left – one of two strategically placed on either side of the village. After another kilometre take the right turn (4km/ N24°47.705' E56°07.342') towards the villages of Jeema and Fay. The road crosses a bridge over Wadi Jeema (6.6km/ N24°47.060' E56°08.686') and, after another 3km, you'll pass a sign welcoming you to the Sultanate of Oman. (Although you'll have entered Oman here, no passports or visas are required for this route.) Keep straight here, through the village of Fay.

The tarmac road merges into a track

Clear water runs through a well-constructed falaj near Hatta Pools.

Shift out of 4x4
and into relaxation mode.

فــندق حــصــن حـتـا
Hatta Fort Hotel

After roughing it in the dunes or the wadis,
why not cruise into the Hatta Fort Hotel for
some rest and relaxation?

Refresh in the cool waters of our unique rock
garden swimming pool.

Recharge with a laid-back, open-air lunch in
our casual Gazebo Coffee Shop.

Relax in Relais & Chateaux accredited luxury.

For more information, call 04 8523211, Fax: 04 8523561,
Email: hfhhotel@emirates.net.ae, Website www.dutcohotels.com

RELAIS &
CHATEAUX.

الــضـيـافـة والامـتـيـاز مـن تـقـالـيـد فـنـادق دتـكـو
DUTCO HOTELS – A TRADITION OF HOSPITALITY AND EXCELLENCE

Hatta Pools is one of the most popular swimming destinations in the region.

after Fay (11.1km/N24°45.510' E56°10.400'). Just before the tarmac ends, there's a turn-off to the right (southwards), which leads to Hatta Pools 6km away. The road crosses several wadis and passes a number of signs to different villages, each of which could provide an interesting detour.

Since there's no shade at Hatta Pools and because they're also further from the track than most people would like to carry

their cool-boxes, you might decide to picnic before reaching the pools. Many side wadis and small oases and villages on either side of the track offer ideal spots. Besides the shade, these places also have fresh running water, lush plantations and the opportunity to meet some of the villagers.

Don't be surprised if you see an old man fishing in one of the ponds along the stream. One villager told the writer he'd

Campers should learn to read the landscape and terrain for warning signs. In the rainy season camp-sites must be chosen with care, away from wadi beds or narrow gorges with a history of flooding. Check the site to see what type of ground you're on. A steep wadi with large boulders and rocks in the ground indicates a flood path.

Also, don't be fooled by clear skies above you. There could

always be a flood on its way, caused by heavy rainfall on the mountain tops just a few kilometres away. Sadly, in one recent incident in the Hatta area, a number of schoolchildren lost their lives when their vehicle was washed away in a flash flood.

Note that wet and marshy regions are unsuitable for camping. Such areas are likely to be infested with mosquitoes and other insects.

been eating fish from this stream for the past 20 years.

Hatta Pools

The turn-off to the pools is on the left-hand side of the road at the wide wadi of Al Qahfi (17km/N24°42.631' E56°10.951'), just after the road descends dramatically towards the wadi. There's no sign of water yet because it's hidden within a smaller wadi further away.

At the turn-off there's a fork where you should turn left and travel no more than 0.6km to a suitable parking place above the pools. If you turn right, however, you can drive down to the beautifully constructed *falaj* nearby to see the crystal-clear water and a fair amount of small fish. There's also a narrow bridge that's just wide enough for most 4x4s, offering an alternative route down to the wadi, about 100m away. You could turn left at the wadi and drive back towards the first of the pools (17.6km/N24°42.827' E56°11.090').

Another way to get closer to the pools is to drive a kilometre further along the main track and take the track marked 'Khamis' (19km/N24°42.210' E56°10.586'). This track takes you to the other side of the wadi from where you can

again drive much closer to the pools.

Walk down along the stream to reach the pools. While walking you'll note the deep, smooth façade and continuous curved surface of the rocks, telling a story of thousands of years of relentless water erosion. The pools change form after each rainfall or flood; some fill up with gravel while new ones come alive. Either way, it's a beautiful place to swim.

Waterfalls

The most exciting part of the outing is yet to come. Once you've enjoyed a dip you can continue downstream on the flat bedrock of the wadi, crossing numerous puddles. After the rains a wide stream emerges from the pool and leads into a narrow gorge. The stream suddenly plunges into this gorge, resulting in waterfalls of different heights. Further downstream the drop is so steep you can hardly see the bottom.

You could continue walking along the top of the canyon following the stream before it finally disappears into the ground. Or you could work your way down to the gorge and walk in the refreshing water between the smooth rocks. Don't forget your camera!

ROUTE 7 RAY AND SURROUNDING VILLAGES

This trip will allow you to explore the inner reaches of the ranges that stretch beyond the Hatta Mountains. You can also visit Ray, A'Shuwayhah and a few smaller hamlets hidden deep within the green wadis at the foot of the high mountains of Al Hajar.

There are four different access routes to this area: from Hatta in the north; via the Madam-Hatta Road, following the direction to Mahda; through Wadi Sumayni to the west; and from Mahda to the south. The route described follows the one most readers will use – from Hatta.

The approach from Hatta
This route passes Hatta Pools so, as mentioned in Route 6, zero your odometer at the Hatta Fort Hotel Roundabout

IN BRIEF

STARTING POINT: Hatta.
FINISHING POINT: Ray.
DISTANCE: 26 km from Hatta to Ray plus approximately 50 km for exploring the surrounding tracks and villages.
TIME REQUIRED: One to one-and-a-half days.
CATEGORY: 4x4.
HIGHLIGHTS: Traditional villages, natural pools, waterfalls, streams, picturesque views of mountain ranges, wadis and oases.

(N24°49.124' E56°08.056') and follow the route to the Hatta Pools turn-off. Although a visit to the pools need not be too time-consuming, it might be advisable to leave this for the return trip. In any case, you'll be heading towards more pools further along the track.

Wadi Al Qahfi
The track from the Hatta Pools turn-off continues in a southwesterly direction into Wadi Al Qahfi, a very wide wadi surrounded by tall mountains. Crossing the wadi, which is often covered by running water, can be exciting – but, although splashing through can be fun, it's best first to check how deep the water is to avoid getting any vulnerable parts of your 4x4 wet.

The track crosses Wadi Al Qahfi (at 18.5km/N24°41.978' E56°10.385') where

The new mosque in Ray has the rugged Hajar Mountains as a backdrop.

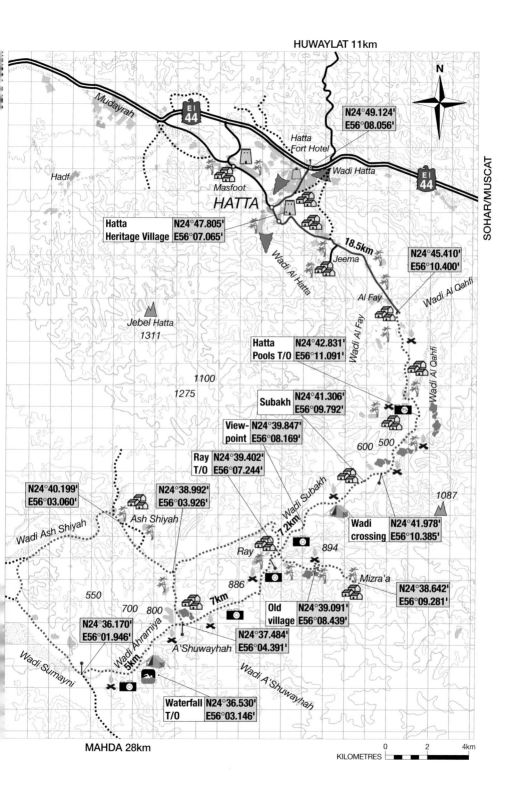

The forces of nature: Interesting rock patterns are a feature of this route.

you can turn right and drive 200m up the wadi to a pool that can get very crowded on Fridays, but might be well worth checking out at other times.

From the pool, return to the main track and continue towards Ray – up and down many hills with numerous large wadis feeding into the main wadi from either side. Some lead to dead ends but others may have an oasis, stream, pond or private picnic spot, while a small village or hamlet could be hidden deep within any of them.

Subakh

Along the way a number of signs lead you to different villages. One of these (at 20.3km/N24°41.306' E56°09.792') is Subakh, located on the right-hand side,

no more than a kilometre beyond the main track. Many of the original residents, especially the younger generation, have been lured to the nearby towns. But on weekends the children return to visit the few elderly members of the family who've stayed behind. Although many young people have relocated, the village still enjoys its natural beauty and the resources that no doubt served its inhabitants for centuries.

There's an interesting mix of old dwellings made of stone, with pitched 'arish' (palm-frond, or barasti) roofs, and modern concrete houses. The brilliant colours of the doors and windows add to the natural beauty of the surroundings. Sadly, in recent years, some of the farmers have been forced to fence off their land because of the influx of visitors.

Some 600m from the turn-off to Subakh, the track crosses Wadi Al Qahfi again (21km/N24°41.172' E56°09.460'). During times of rain, there might be water in the wadi. A formal camp-site was being constructed some 300m beyond this crossing at the time of writing. Further on, the track reaches a high point (at 24.7km/N24°39.847' E56°08.169') from where there's a spectacular view across the wadi, and after another kilometre there's a turn-off to the village of Ray (25.7km/N24°39.402' E56°07.244').

Ray

Ray is scenically located in Wadi Al Qahfi's wide sand-and-gravel bed. Blessed with good soil and water, the village is one of the most prosperous in the area. Many locals have moved into the village and built houses there after abandoning inaccessible settlements deep inside the rugged mountains.

Here too the villagers are friendly and, after an exchange of greetings, you may be lucky enough to be invited for a cup of

Arabic coffee and some fruit. If so, perhaps a few simple inquiries about the area will help keep you on the right path in the midst of many confusing tracks.

Several tracks converging at Ray run southwards to A'Shuwayhah, north to Ash Shiyah and east to Mizra'a.

Mizra'a (A'Da'inah)

This charming village (see separate box) is located 5km up a dead-end track leading east into the heart of the mountains – a fertile area fed by springs (N24°38.642' E56°09.281'). Lush palm groves and plantations bear many fruits including pomegranates, grapefruits, lemons, oranges, bananas and grapes – there's even coffee – all terraced down to the wadi and fed from the falaj and the stream above. Nowadays a gate placed a few hundred metres away from the village blocks the way.

The scenic route along Wadi Al Qahfi, between Hatta and A'Shuwayhah.

VILLAGE PEOPLE

The village of Mizra'a is home to Salim bin Ka'ab, his wife Miryam and their four sons. Their daughters-in-law and many grand-children can also be seen carrying out their daily duties. The family is so large that, to the first-time visitor, it may seem to be more than just one family.

Now in their newly-built home, the bin Ka'ab clan enjoys modern facilities such as a generator for electricity. The framed photo of HM Sultan Qaboos on the wall is a reminder that you're in Oman.

The older sons work in Mahda but keep their families in the village and try to provide them with some of the luxuries from town to soften the hardships of rural life. It's the old man's wish to keep the family together and carry on the tradition of his forefathers in this isolated village. He's not too sure how long it will be before his sons finally move to the city but knows that day is not too far off.

Abandoned village

An abandoned village lies on the plateau across the wadi, halfway towards Mizra'a from Ray. To walk through this village is to take a trip into the past. The remains tell the story of the ingenuity of its inhabitants and their resourcefulness in harnessing nature and adapting to the harshness of the environs.

However, it's not that easy to reach. Look for a track on your right going into the wadi as soon as the village is spotted on the horizon. Work your way down the wadi on the very steep track and drive upstream on the wadi bed across large boulders. After a few hundred metres you'll catch sight of luxuriant green palms along the wadi, leading to a lush oasis filled with all types of fruits, especially lemons, tangerines and, of course, dates. Even though you may not find anybody here, it's obvious that the groves are still well cared for.

To reach the village, you have to walk up the oasis on the path under the shady trees to the water-holes, then climb out of the wadi on steps actually carved into the rocks by the residents of the village.

On the plateau, the numerous remains

of houses indicate the extent of this once-flourishing settlement. Dwellings are of a stone base with sloped palm-frond roofs. Although most of the houses appear to be abandoned, many are kept locked and seem well cared for and frequently visited.

A'Shuwayhah

Back on the main track, just 7km southwest of Ray and very similar to it, A'Shuwayhah (N24°37.484' E56°04.391') enjoys year-round running water from the wadi stream; it also has rich agricultural land and a mosque. This village is made of scattered

houses with colourful doors. Ask any child playing around the village, and he'll show you the pools that are the lifeblood of the village and the gardens below.

The route to A'Shuwayhah is very picturesque, with the track crossing the wadi on several occasions. From A'Shuwayhah the track continues southwest into Wadi Ahramiya and Wadi Sumayni, and north to Ash Shiyah.

Waterfall

On the way to Wadi Sumayni, 3km from A'Shuwayhah, a track to the left leads towards a waterfall (N24°36.530' E56°03.146'). This track has not been well maintained and needs careful negotiation. After 1km and two wadi crossings, you'll reach the wadi in which the waterfall is situated.

You'll know you're in the right place when you can't drive any further. Park in the wadi and walk up the stream to the left for about 100m until you reach the waterfall. Moss has grown on the rocks and there's an abundance of oleanders in the area.

In a wet season the flow is quite strong and the pool below is deep, making it an ideal spot to have a dip, while climbing above the fall and wading up the stream provides good exercise and an unforgettable experience.

Return journey

There are several options for the return journey. The fastest way is probably to go back to Hatta. Alternatively you can head south towards Mahda and Al Ain, or go west through Wadi Sumayni. Whichever route you select, make sure you have enough time to make your way out of the area before dark to minimise the risk of getting lost.

This scenic waterfall is a short drive from the village of A'Shuwayhah.

ROUTE 8 KHATWA

As indicated in the panel, this is an easy route with a number of highlights, one of them being the excitement of visiting Oman without the hassle of passports and visas. Buraimi is a fascinating, historical oasis town that – with its souk (market), forts and oasis – is a great place to explore before proceeding to Khatwa.

Khatwa, set in a verdant oasis, has the relaxed atmosphere of a bygone era, with the added advantage of friendly people. Travelling along this route is like taking a step back in time and it provides an ideal opportunity to observe the different dress and customs of a neighbouring country.

IN BRIEF

STARTING POINT: Buraimi.
FINISHING POINT: Buraimi (round trip).
DISTANCE: 98km.
TIME REQUIRED: Half a day to a full day.
CATEGORY: Possible in a normal saloon car. Easy travelling and mostly on tarmac roads, except within Khatwa village.
HIGHLIGHTS: Old forts, houses and villages at Buraimi, Mahda and Khatwa. Palm groves, *aflaj* and deep gorges with running water in Khatwa.

How to get there

Although Buraimi adjoins Al Ain, the former is in Oman and the latter in the UAE. These two centres used to be separate oasis villages that were major crossroads for caravans travelling from east to west and from north to east (and vice versa), between the Arabian Gulf and the Gulf of Oman. They also functioned as important supply centres for the villages along the western foothills of the Hajar Mountains.

The Buraimi souk, located along the main street in Buraimi, offers not only shopping for the journey but a taste of history as well. There are also two splendid forts, one immediately adjacent to the souk and the other about half a kilometre south of the main road.

The oasis of Khatwa is a good place to leave your car and enjoy a stroll.

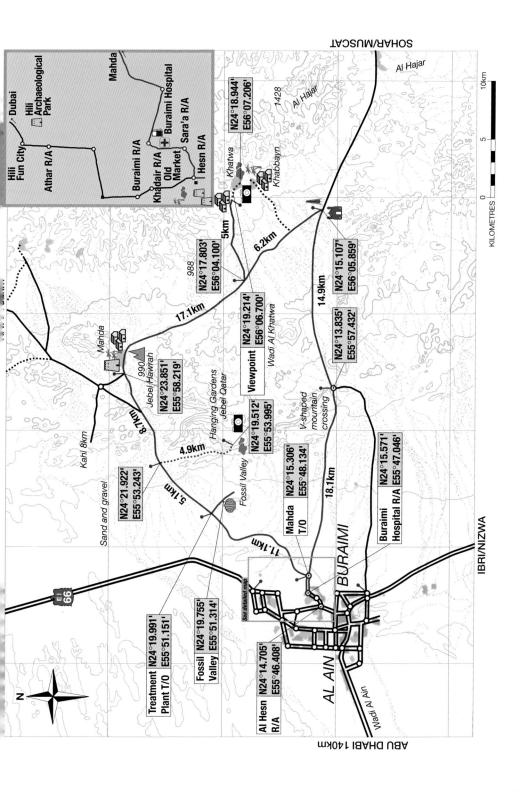

The old oasis and village is to the right of the souk, behind the first fort. With its flowing *aflaj*, wells, old mud walls and winding pathways shaded by palm, citrus, fig, banana and mango trees, it's another place with an atmosphere reminiscent of days gone by – far removed from the hustle and bustle of the modern town.

A stroll down the public paths that lead through the oasis is highly recommended (although you should note that men do bathe in the area), while the newly renovated fort just south of the old souk is also well worth visiting.

Khatwa, located east of Al Ain, is accessible via two routes. The quickest is along the Sohar Road, turning left towards Mahda. However, our route – which makes the most of the area – is a circular one, taking in Buraimi, Mahda, Khatwa and the Sohar–Al Ain Road back to Buraimi.

Take the exit signposted Sa'raa at the Al Hesn Roundabout in front of the souk (N24°14.705' E55°46.408'). At the next

roundabout turn left, following the sign to Al Khadraa Al Jadidah. Then at the next roundabout, the Buraimi Hospital Roundabout (N24°15.570' E55°47.046'), zero your odometer and turn right towards Al Jizi and Sohar. After about 2km travelling eastwards on the Sohar Road you'll see a power station on the left and then the Mahda Road; turn left on to the Mahda Road (N24°15.306' E55°48.134') and drive in a northeasterly direction. (For a more detailed description of driving through Al Ain and Buraimi from the Dubai road side of Al Ain, see the directions at the end of this chapter.)

Fossil Valley

If you enjoy searching for fossils, turn right (eastwards), at a sign saying 'Sewage Treatment Plant' (13.1km/N24°19.991' E55°51.151'), into a large bowl surrounded by a low mountain range. From here you should see the imposing peaks of Jebel Qatar about 5km to the east. Drive for another 550m on the

These old ruins are situated behind the renovated fort near Buraimi souk.

tarmac road along the side of the bowl, park your vehicle and get out to look for fossils along the ridge of rocks to your right (N24°19.755' E55°51.314').

This area is known as Fossil Valley and has many fascinating types of marine fossils. As tempting as it may be, remember to take only photographs and leave only footprints. If only a few people plunder fossil sites, there'll soon be nothing left for anyone to see.

Hanging Gardens

After visiting Fossil Valley, drive out of the valley and return to the tar road going to Mahda. Disregarding any kilometres for the detour, after 18.2km (N24°21.922' E55°53.243') turn right on to a track which proceeds through a gravel plain. This leads to the parking spot for Hanging Gardens 4.9km away (N24°19.512' E55°53.995'). As you approach the parking spot (next to a shady tree and a large boulder), you'll notice the Hanging Gardens on the slopes to your right.

Attractions at the approach to the Hanging Gardens include natural pools at intervals along the wadi, a variety of vegetation including water plants and interesting rock formations. Best of all is the panoramic view of the Hanging Gardens with the vertical cliffs of Jebel Qatar – the trees growing in cracks in the cliffs and hanging from them have to be seen to be believed. There are a number of hiking trails and rock-climbing routes in this area for all levels of fitness.

Mahda

Back on the tarmac, the next point of interest is the growing town and oasis of Mahda (26.9km/N24°23.851' E55°58.219'). Mahda makes an interesting stopover. An old caravan post with a great

wealth of water and soil on the alluvial plains of Jebel Al Gharb, it was also a stronghold for neighbouring tribes and today has much to offer the visitor.

Although it's been developed recently and modern houses have appeared, Mahda hasn't lost the intrinsic character of an authentic Omani village. After working your way through the more developed areas on the outskirts, you'll reach the old village where mud houses still stand together with two forts and several watch-towers, which are easily accessible.

There are also several palm plantations with fortifications around them and a central oasis, rich and green, overshadowed by the Jebel Hawrah standing 990m above sea level. This is the catchment area for all the water that comes down from the nearby mountains and the reason why Mahda is such a green and popular town.

The Hanging Gardens are scenically situated among the cliffs of Jebel Qatar.

Khatwa

The circular route continues towards the old village of Khatwa, the highlight of this route and a place where you could spend the whole day. From Mahda, drive in a southeasterly direction and you'll find the link road to Khatwa on the left (at 44km/N24°17.803' E 56°04.100'). This runs northeastwards towards the mountains for 5km.

On the way you'll see the new village of Khatwa, which contrasts sharply with what you're going to see further on. Drive slowly as you reach the top of the steep pass, otherwise you'll miss a superb panoramic view of the oasis and the village (at 49.3km/N24°19.217' E56°06.700').

Continue into the oasis and village. The track is narrow and at its end you'll see an open space near a small mosque (N24°18.944' E56°07.206'). Leave your vehicle here and proceed further on foot, down the quiet and tranquil path surrounded by gardens irrigated by a *falaj* system carrying clear running water. It's a beautiful walk and the villagers expect visitors to respect their privacy and keep the area clean. There used to be a sign warning people not to use soap in the *aflaj* water since it's used for irrigation.

As you work your way through the palm plantations and fruit gardens towards the wadi, pause to look at the houses, constructed in the traditional manner of mud and stone with *'arish* (palm-frond, or *barasti*) roofs.

From the mosque, keep to the left along the main *falaj* for about 200m, then turn right (ie southwards) and walk down the plantation towards a deep, narrow gorge. Listen carefully and you'll understand how the gorge was created. Over the years, a continuous flow of water

has cut through more than 50m of rock.

Sections of the gorge's walls have crumbled, making entry into the gorge possible in places further east. It may also be crossed by means of a concrete footbridge. A short walk, crossing a few more gorges, will take you to the village of Khabbayn on the other side.

To complete your discovery of Khatwa Oasis, drive back to the entrance and then down to the wadi (N24°18.944' E56°07.206'). You'll notice the intricate stone walls built to protect the trees from floods and to provide narrow terraces for growing crops. In many places, the palm trees shading the narrow wadi provide interesting photo opportunities.

Return journey

Take the track back to the main tarmac road and head southeastwards towards the main Sohar Road. Turn right, on to the Sohar Road (65km/N24°15.107' E56°05.859') and proceed westwards towards Buraimi. Turn right at the roundabout (79.9km/N24°13.835' E55°57.432') and drive through the V-shaped cut in the mountain and back to the Hospital Roundabout (98km/ N24°15.570' E55°47.046').

Finding your way through Al Ain and Buraimi to Fossil Valley and the Hanging Gardens

These directions are for the approach from Dubai. If you're travelling from Abu Dhabi, follow the signs to Al Ain town centre and then to Buraimi, where you can link up with this route.

0km: Arriving at the outskirts of Al Ain, zero your odometer at the first (Oha) roundabout, known as the Coffee Pot Roundabout, and continue straight along Emirates Street.

2.8km: Continue straight at the next (2nd) roundabout.

5.3km: At the next (3rd) roundabout, Hili Fun City Roundabout, turn left towards Hili Archaelogical Park. (At Hili Fun City you can see a massive

The little pass that descends into Khatwa is spectacularly beautiful.

DATE-PALM OASES

The date-harvesting season is from June to the end of October. There are many different varieties of dates, with different types being harvested at different times.

In bygone years oasis farmers depended on the ubiquitous date palm as much as the nomadic Bedouin depended on the camel. The date palm produces fruit that's rich in calories and is easily preserved. It also produces timber. Virtually every part of the tree can be used: the trunks to make columns and ceilings for houses, and the fronds for roofs and walls, as well as bags, brooms, mats and fans. The seeds are used to feed livestock, and the wood is burned for fuel.

Perhaps most importantly, the date palm was essential for the agriculture of the entire oasis, since it created the microclimate necessary for the cultivation of other plants.

Recently, however, the hardy date palm's importance as a provider of shade has declined. Modern methods of preservation, coupled with the availability of imported food, has also led to changes and variety in the diet of rural people, so the significance of the date palm has lessened – in the same way as that of the camel.

However, it still retains its symbolic significance, and is widely used to break the fast during the month of Ramadan.

---

reconstructed tomb from the late third millennium BC, among many other archaeological treasures.)

6.3km: Continue straight at the next (4th) roundabout, Athar Roundabout.

7.8km: Turn right into Bani Yas Street at the next (5th) roundabout.

9.4km: Turn left into Al Falah Street (ie towards Hili Industrial Area) at traffic lights.

10.6km: Continue straight at the next (6th) roundabout, into Oman.

11.2km: Continue straight at the next (7th) roundabout, into Buraimi.

12.7km: Pass the entrance to the old souk, situated next to Buraimi Fort. The oasis and *falaj*, with traces of old dwellings, mosques and walls, lie beyond the souk.

13.1km: Turn left towards Sa'raa at the next (8th) roundabout, known as Al Hesn Roundabout.

14km: Turn left towards the village of Khadra at the next (9th) roundabout,

the Sa'raa Roundabout.

15.6km: Turn right towards Al Jizi/Sohar at the next (10th) roundabout, the Hospital Roundabout. There's a large mosque next to this roundabout as well as a petrol station – your last chance to fill up and buy food and water for some distance.

17.6km: Turn left towards Mahdah at the next (11th) roundabout

29.3km: Turn right towards Fossil Valley – at a sign saying 'Sewage Treatment Plant' – on to a tar road. There's a ridge of rocks to the right of this road and this is one of the places where you can search for fossils.

34.3km (excluding any detour into Fossil Valley): Turn right on to a track which proceeds through a gravel plain. This leads to the parking spot for Hanging Gardens, **4.9km** away. As you approach the parking spot (next to a shady tree and a large boulder) you'll notice the Hanging Gardens to the left of a large cave on the slopes to your right.

Wadi Al Khadra is a relatively short wadi that carries floodwaters from the Hajar Mountains down to Wadi Sharm, from where they disappear into the gravel plains beyond Nuway. The sudden changes of elevation in the rocky wadi bed have created several waterfalls and pools along the way, and given rise to some spectacular vistas.

There are also a number of picturesque wadis, villages and oases in this area.

The wadi and village of Sharm

Some 20 years ago there was a fully-fledged village in Sharm. Now, with new houses being built in nearby Nuway, most of the villagers have left Sharm. But some inhabitants have chosen to stay in the tranquil old village rather than move to more modern surroundings.

It's an area of great beauty, encompassing the foothills of the Hajar Mountains, flood plains and rocky gravel hills where the rich-yet-subdued colours of the vegetation stand out against the red, white and brown hues of the gravel-and-sand backdrop.

The village has an old fort in fairly good condition, surrounded by stone dwellings. The fort is typical of old forts in the area. Located on high ground, its stone walls stand at various levels and it's easy to see how it once protected the area as it overlooks not only the village, but an expanse of farmland, palm plantations and the wadi itself.

> ## IN BRIEF
>
> **STARTING POINT:** Buraimi.
> **FINISHING POINT:** Wadi Khadra.
> **DISTANCE:** 75km.
> **TIME REQUIRED:** One day.
> **CATEGORY:** 4x4.
> **HIGHLIGHTS:** The old villages and atmospheric oases of Mahda, Sharm and Khadra, and Khadra Pools.

Wadi Sharm in flood: Off-road drivers should always be alert for flash floods.

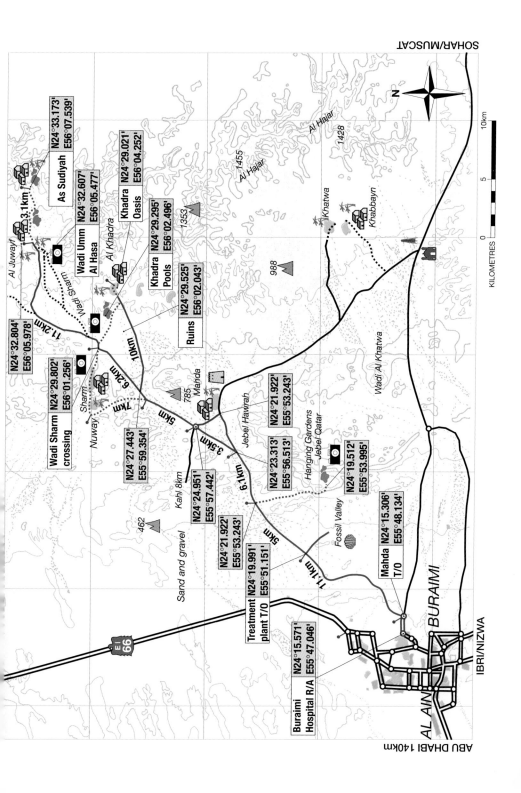

Take a step back in time in Buraimi Oasis, situated behind the town's souk.

As in a number of other villages in the area, the *falaj* system is still in use, with a continuous flow of water feeding the farms, while the houses are clustered together in the village with the farms surrounding them.

In contrast to most other wadis, this one is visited by townfolk from both Oman and the UAE. They enjoy picnics in the parts of the wadi that cut through the mountains, or within the shady date-palm plantations.

Sharm is one of the widest wadis in the region and has a good supply of water, especially during winter when it gushes

Wadi Sharm after a flood – part of the village of Sharm can also be seen.

down from the Hajar Mountains into the wadi and follows its course on to the plains beyond Nuway where the sand and gravel absorb the water.

In addition to visiting Wadi Sharm you could also go in a northeasterly direction to Al Juwayf, one of the greenest spots in the area. Juwayf is situated on a plain with both old and new homes and a mosque surrounded by mountains. On the return journey, after passing Al Juwayf, you could go into Wadi Hallaheh to enjoy some mountain rambling.

How to get to Wadi Sharm

Zero your odometer at the Buraimi Hospital Roundabout (N24°15.571' E55°47.046') and follow the route to Mahda (see Route 8). If you have the time, you can visit Fossil Valley (also featured in Route 8) and Jebel Qatar and the Hanging Gardens.

Continue towards Mahda, departing

from the main road at a fork (at 23km/N24°23.313' E55°56.513'). After almost 4km more (27.7km/N24°24.951' E55°57.442'), still on tarmac, you'll reach a small roundabout. Left takes you to Kahl and right to Mahda, but our route continues straight towards Wadi Sharm.

On the way, you'll see several signs, such as 'Nuway 7 kilometres' (at 32.7km) and 'Al Khadra 10 kilometres' (at 33.2km). Nevertheless, continue driving to where the road goes down into Wadi Sharm (38.2km/N24°29.802' E56°01.256'). Turn left (westwards) into the wadi and travel down the wadi for 3.2km to reach the village of Sharm.

If you turn right (eastwards) instead of left towards the village, the wadi branches out into several tributaries. A drive into any of these smaller wadis could produce many places of natural beauty and some great picnic spots, one of them being the pools at Khadra.

How to get to Juwayf

If you don't turn into Wadi Sharm but continue in a northeasterly direction you'll reach Al Juwayf. At present the tarmac road ends at Al Juwayf (49.4km/N24°32.804' E56°05.978'). A well-graded track from Al Juwayf proceeds to As Sudiyah village, a beautiful oasis with deep gorges and old huts in the foothills of the forbidding Al Hajar Al Gharbi Mountain to the east (52.5km/ N24°33.173' E56°07.539'). From here you cannot proceed any further, unless of course on foot.

Numerous wadis such as Wadi Hallalah, Wadi Muzayrab and Wadi Sada carry the rainwater from this mountain to Wadi Sharm. *En route* to Al Juwayf – on the right-hand side just a few metres off the tarmac road – you'll notice a magnificent canyon, Wadi Umm Al Hasa, the meeting point of these wadis, best seen after a heavy flooding

(N24°32.607' E56°05.477').

Beyond Juwayf, towards the mountain, there are several pools ideal for swimming in and picnicking by.

How to get to Khadra Pools

There are several ways to get to Khadra Pools but our route starts from the tarmac road from Mahda to Juwayf. This road crosses Wadi Sharm 38.2km from the Buraimi Hospital Roundabout. Zero your odometer here and turn right into the wadi bed.

You'll immediately notice many dying palms – a sad indication of how the water-table has dropped in recent years. Continue up the wadi to a fork some 200m further on (0.2km/N24°29.814' E56°01.359'), where you take the right-hand (minor) track in a southeasterly direction. After a further 100m turn right on to a barely discernible track that takes you out of the wadi (0.3km/N24°29.796' E56°01.439'); at the time of writing (2002), this track was also partly hidden from vision by dying palms.

The drive out of the wadi is steep and very rough and will require low-range 4x4 driving. A sharp, steep right followed by a left turn takes you to the top of the wadi and a fairly flat plateau. From here the driving is relatively smooth on a hard track, well marked by passing vehicles.

Intriguing ruins

A puzzling phenomenon on this section is the remains of an unknown settlement spread over a large area. These are the lower sections of walls, one-half to one metre in width and approximately a metre in height (1.5km/N24°29.525' E56°02.043'). The large enclosures sport square and rectangular spaces, some 10–20 metres long, which could not have

At Khadra Pools you can enjoy cool water and amazing rock formations.

been the rooms of houses since no roof would have been able to support such large spans. The enclosures are oriented in a similar direction and are separated from each other by intermediate spaces.

The rocks are placed in layers in a methodical manner, indicating the refined technical skills of the builders. Strangest, perhaps, is the selection of the site, nowhere near the fertile land its inhabitants would need for agricultural pursuits, but possibly the pools at Khadra were the reason for its existence.

The plateau continues with mountains visible on the horizon in subdued shades of blue and magenta. The sky seems vast and the quiet plateau gives a feeling of loneliness. Soon you'll reach a fork (2.2km) where you take the left track towards the wadi. Continue for another 300m or so to a level area where tyre marks indicate a place of interest (2.5km/N24°29.295' E56°02.496'). Another conspicuous landmark here is the electrical cables crossing the wadi.

Leave your 4x4 here and take one of the two paths that wind down to the wadi. Although nothing can be seen from the top, before you're halfway down you'll see a cave gouged into the wadi wall and, in front of it, a pool.

Khadra Pools

As you continue downwards on the path you'll notice the remains of a *falaj* carved into the edge of the wadi wall. The method of construction and sophisticated material used indicates an ingenious skill similar to that exhibited at the ruins passed earlier and this *falaj* may well have been the watercourse for that settlement.

While descending you'll also notice steps purposely cut into the rock. They add to the mystery but may have provided access to the pools for people living on the plateau during times of drought, when the *falaj* was dry.

A well-graded track takes you deep into the verdant oasis of Khadra.

The extent of the pool and the falls behind them (when flowing) can't be seen until you get down to the pool itself. Depending on the depth of the pool in a particular season, access to the cave may be through the water.

The size of the pool and the waterfall varies according to the quantity of rainfall during the season, while the depth is also related to the accumulation of gravel. In a dry year the pool becomes a small pond. When the water is low in a dry season you may even feel gentle nips from fish living in the water. There are also toads, lizards on the rock walls, and a number of birds coming to drink at this delightful spot.

Almost hidden at one end of the pool is an entrance to a narrow gorge. A swim upstream through the gorge is quite an experience, giving the feeling of a voyage of discovery into a seemingly never-ending world of darkness. The gorge becomes narrower and higher until the sky is only a strip of light high above you. The water is crystal-clear and deep and the gorge so narrow that in some places you can touch both sides of the gorge simultaneously.

Venturing to the end of the gorge is an experience that shouldn't be missed. After the initial swim you'll reach some large boulders and a gravel path. Continue walking (and swimming, if necessary) upstream until you reach another watercourse ending in a deep pool with water gushing into it from a hole above.

Although there's much to see, it takes only a few minutes to get from the pool at the cave to the final point. If you want to use your camera here you'll need to take a waterproof bag and a float, while suitable aquatic shoes or sandals are strongly recommended to protect your feet.

The path above the pool

Before leaving the pools, you can work your way upstream along the side of the gorge until you reach a stream with beautifully carved rocks in its bed. At times you can see and hear the water gushing out from among the rocks. If you're adventurous enough you may want to look for the source of the water. You may also notice that the *falaj* seen earlier on the wadi wall is now curved into the wadi bed. If you keep on the track above the wadi you'll eventually reach Khadra.

The route from Khadra Pools to Khadra Oasis

From the parking spot above the pools, continue further along the track until you reach a tarmac road (4.7km/N24°28.628' E56°03.237'). Turn left on to this road

PHOTOGRAPHY

Winter is the ideal time for photography in the desert, mountains and wadis of the Emirates. The sky is blue and the air is clear, resulting in crisp and bright images. Three things are vital to good landscape photography. **Composition:** Vast expanses hold many small surprises. Remember to look at the details in things such as plants, the ripples in the sand and rock strata. Every colour is enhanced against a dull, barren landscape. If you look hard enough you'll see a pretty pattern.

Time of day: The best time for landscape photography is in the early morning or late afternoon. When the temperature is lower, the light is subdued and the colours are warmer. Midday gives a bluish, hazy hue to pictures and in winter you get a good contrast of bright colours. Try a light-blue filter for the late afternoon to cancel the extreme warmth of the light while an amber filter at midday will enhance the warmth.

A polarising filter enriches the colour of the sky. The sunny, tranquil days of winter are a photographer's dream. Stormy days can produce some dramatic images, but take care not to expose your camera and lenses to blowing sand. The consequences of this could be scratches on your film or, worse still, expensive repairs to your equipment.
Subject matter: Intriguing forms and patterns can be found in the desert. Visual distortions and mirages can also be artistically exploited. Because of its vastness, smoothness and depth, even the smallest detail stands out in the desert.

In summer, the extreme heat outdoors can spoil your film. A cool-box is recommended to carry and store both used and unused films. Slide film is more susceptible to the effects of heat than colour-negative film for prints. Sunrise and sunsets in the desert are dramatic, while capturing the play of the moonlight can create amazing images.

---

and, after 200m or so, the tarmac ends at the entrance to Khadra Oasis.

The village and oasis of Khadra are picturesque and worth exploring. A well-graded track beyond the wadi crossing continues deep into the verdant oasis, exposing the wealth and richness of Khadra (6.5km/N24°29.021' E56°04.252'). In this densely planted oasis you'll notice, in addition to the palms, several types of fruit trees.

The water in this wadi flows all year round so be careful not to get stuck – especially if you're in a saloon car. Incidentally, this water feeds into the Khadra Pools further down the wadi.

Direct approach to Khadra (from the Mahda–Wadi Sharm Road)

If you're not approaching the oasis from the pools, about 5.5km from the roundabout in Mahda, on the right-hand side travelling towards Juwayf, a signpost '10 kilometres to Khadra' (N24°27.443' E55°59.354') guides you to the village of Khadra.

By following another signpost, you can also detour to Al Rumaitha, where there are several water pools 3km away.

You can return to Buraimi along the same route or, if you want to explore further, you could continue northwards towards Hatta or Wadi Sumaini.

ROUTE 10 HATTA–BURAIMI

The Hatta–Mahda route incorporates three shorter routes: Hatta Pools (route 6), Ray and surrounding villages (route 7) and Wadi Sharm and Khadra (route 9). It's a long drive so, if you want to complete it in a day, plan an early start.

An ideal way to make the most of this route is to camp overnight above one of the wadis and start early the following morning. The two major starting points of this route are Hatta from the north or Al Ain from the south.

Starting from Al Ain

If your starting point is Al Ain, follow the route to Buraimi, Mahda and Wadi Sharm (see routes 8 and 9), then continue north to Shuwayhah and Ray

IN BRIEF

STARTING POINT: Hatta or Al Ain.
FINISHING POINT: Al Ain or Hatta.
DISTANCE: 100km.
TIME: One to one-and-a-half days or more.
CATEGORY: 4x4.
HIGHLIGHTS: Old forts and settlements, camping and picnicking spots, waterfalls and pools, and interesting detours.

and northeast to Hatta Pools and finally Hatta village. Other routes take you through Wadi Sumayni and then either to Shuaib or north to the Hatta–Dubai road. Whichever route you decide on calculate the time you'll need to complete the trip and join a main road before night falls.

Starting from Hatta

For mileages, refer to the table at the end of this chapter. Follow the directions for Hatta Pools where you can enjoy swimming in several pools in Wadi Qahfi before reaching Ray. Walking along wadis, climbing the hills or exploring some of the pools along the way is a rewarding experience (see route 6). Beyond Hatta Pools, Ray and the

The drive through Wadi Qahfi is not difficult, unless done after a heavy flood.

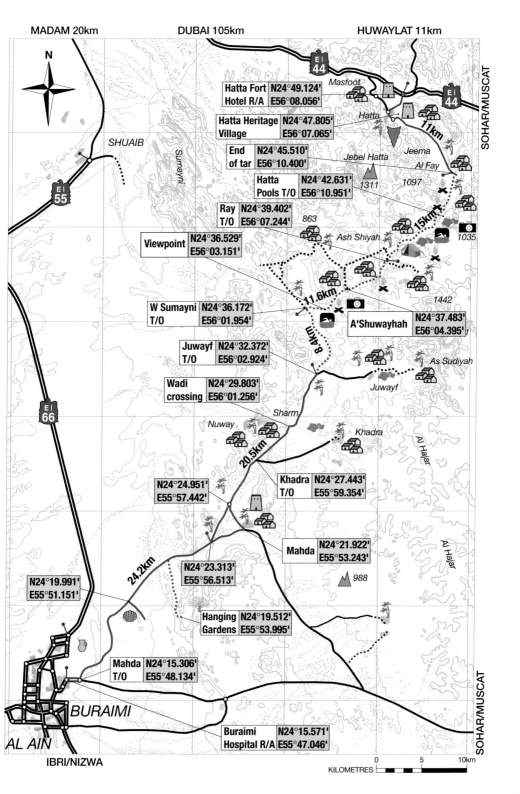

MADAM 20km   DUBAI 105km   HUWAYLAT 11km

N

SHUAIB

Sumayni

Masfoot

Hatta

Jeema
Al Fay

Jebel Hatta

1311   1097

863

Ash Shiyah

1035

1442

As Sudiyah

Juwayf

Sharm

Nuway

Khadra

Al Hajar

Al Hajar

988

BURAIMI

AL AIN

IBRI/NIZWA

SOHAR/MUSCAT

SOHAR/MUSCAT

Hatta Fort Hotel R/A	N24°49.124' E56°08.056'
Hatta Heritage Village	N24°47.805' E56°07.065'
End of tar	N24°45.510' E56°10.400'
Hatta Pools T/O	N24°42.631' E56°10.951'
Ray T/O	N24°39.402' E56°07.244'
Viewpoint	N24°36.529' E56°03.151'
W Sumayni T/O	N24°36.172' E56°01.954'
A'Shuwayhah	N24°37.483' E56°04.395'
Juwayf T/O	N24°32.372' E56°02.924'
Wadi crossing	N24°29.803' E56°01.256'
Khadra T/O	N24°27.443' E55°59.354'
	N24°24.951' E55°57.442'
Mahda	N24°21.922' E55°53.243'
	N24°23.313' E55°56.513'
	N24°19.991' E55°51.151'
Hanging Gardens	N24°19.512' E55°53.995'
Mahda T/O	N24°15.306' E55°48.134'
Buraimi Hospital R/A	N24°15.571' E55°47.046'

11km
15km
11.6km
8.4km
20.5km
24.2km

0   5   10km
KILOMETRES

surrounding villages also offer several picnicking and hiking areas (route 7).

From Ray, continue in a southwesterly direction to Shuwayhah (N24°37.483' E56°04.395'), through Wadi Ahramiya, until you reach Wadi Sumayni, where there's a good viewpoint (at N24°36.529' E56°03.151'). Driving along Wadi Shuwayhah and exploring its lush green oasis should not be missed. The waterfall a short drive from here can be unforgettable if you catch it in a wet season (see route 7).

While in Wadi Sumayni drive southeast down the track. This brings you to the end of the wadi, where mountains give way to gravel plains at the Juwayf turn-off in Wadi Sharm. Here, many of the smaller wadis that bring the floods down from the mountains to the west converge.

At this turn-off the roads lead south

A typical decorated door at Juwayf; the mountains are even more attractive.

towards Mahda and east to Juwayf, an oasis located 5km away. Up to this point the journey has been on rough gravel tracks but on reaching the Juwayf road the remainder of the journey is on tarmac – unless you decide on further exploration around Sharm.

Sharm

There's much to explore around Sharm, including Sharm village, Khadra Pools, Khadra village and trekking along the many smaller wadis leading to Wadi Sharm (see routes 8 and 9).

On reaching Wadi Sharm the track descends to a wide gravel wadi bed that usually has running water. This area is one of the most interesting of the whole trip. If you're heading towards Mahda the shortest way is to drive out of the wadi bed and head in a southeasterly direction for 15km, but it would be better to explore several routes in the area before continuing your journey.

Turning east into the first, smaller wadi bed takes you along an interesting

The Hatta–Buraimi Route cuts into the heart of the Hajar Mountains.

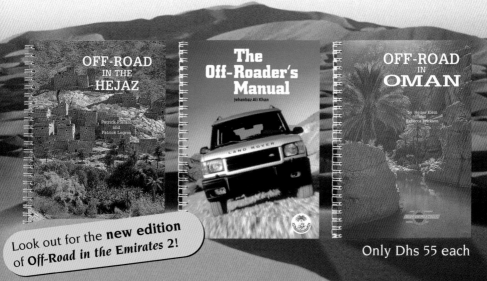

CUSTOMS AND HABITS

Rural people are different from city dwellers the world over. In the UAE, those who live in the countryside tend to be intimate and hospitable and they expect the same courtesy from visitors. They're also territorial and have a strong sense of ownership.

Like the mountains and deserts where they live, they are mysterious and not easy to understand. For their part, they'll wonder why you've come to visit their barren land and look at you suspiciously. It takes a great deal of contact and communication to win their friendship, but if you do it will be for life.

A typical meeting begins with lengthy greetings and handshakes, followed by the exchange of pleasantries. If the conversation carries on they will enquire as to the purpose of your visit and where you're heading.

You may be invited into their house; more often though a mat is brought outside and placed under the shade of the porch. Visitors are often offered fruit, especially dates, accompanied bv tea and coffee brought out in large trays. Fruit is peeled for the guest and the flow of coffee continues. Women are not as inhibited here as they are in the city. Even though we may see them behind a mask or burqa (they may be shy of men) they may go to the extent of shaking hands with them and exchanging pleasantries. Nevertheless, the men and women are often segregated even in one house.

You could be invited to share a meal with the family. Meals are almost always arranged on the floor with the food brought in on large trays and placed on a plastic tablecloth or mat. Everyone approaches the pile of rice topped with meat, chicken or fish, from their own corner. Side dishes include salad, pickled fruits, vegetables and, of course, dates. Water and soft drinks are served during the meal. As a guest, you'll be served the best portions. When the meal is over water is brought in a pitcher to wash the hands. Fruit is then passed around again, accompanied by sweets, tea and coffee.

At the end of the meal everyone retires for a short rest and this is the time to leave. These villagers will never forget you, and will appreciate your visiting them again, especially with any pictures you may have taken of them.

Village people are very traditional in their thinking and have strict social and moral codes. You should be careful not to offend them in any way when you meet them. In return for their hospitality, the least one can do is respect their customs and traditions and perhaps offer them some soft drinks, fruit or other delicacies from the city.

Villagers are always curious about city folk – don't be alarmed if they ask you about your private life! Some of the younger villagers may even be able to speak English.

track past palm plantations, running water and the narrow, straight walls of the wadi (the starting point is at N24°29.803' E56°01.257'). This is an ideal place for picnicking and taking dips in the small water pools.

Travelling west along the gravel wadi bed for a couple of kilometres will take you first to the oasis of Sharm (N24°29.676' E56°00.155') and then to Nuway (N24°29.474' E55°58.689'). Here you'll see the *falaj* running along the wall of the wadi and into the palm groves rising above the edge of the wadi bed.

This is another pleasant picnicking spot.

A visit to the old stone-and-mud fort just off the wadi and a walk through the old village and palm garden will be long remembered. Another spot, also not to be missed, is Wadi Khadra, which takes you through ruins, ancient dwellings of unknown date and finally to the waterfall and pools described in route 9.

Mahda

From Wadi Sharm a new tarmac road takes you south towards the large Omani oasis town of Madha, 15km away. While there, you can visit the old village where the ruins of two old forts and the walled oasis attached to the ruined mud houses tell stories of better times.

The quickest route from Mahda to Al Ain is to take the road in a southwesterly direction towards the centre of Buraimi.

Kilometre counts for Hatta–Buraimi trip

0 km: Hatta Fort Hotel Roundabout.
10.7km: Turn off-road after Fay.
16.2km: Hatta Pools and Wadi Qahfi.
26km: Ray.
31.7km: Shuwayhah.
37.6km: Left turn at Wadi Sumayni.
46km: Back to tarmac road, junction of Sharm to Juwayf.
51km: Juwayf.
62km: Wadi Sharm crossing, add 6km return to Khadra Pools.
68km: Access to Al Khadra village.
73km: Roundabout at Mahda (where you can take a 1km detour to Mahda or an 8km detour to Kahl); continue straight.
76.5km: Junction Buraimi–Mahda, continue straight.
98.8km: Joins Sohar Road. Turn west.
100.7km: Buraimi Hospital Roundabout.

This magnificiently restored fort is situated 600 metres south of the souk at Buraimi.

ROUTE 11 HATTA–MUNAY–KHOR KALBA

Because of its proximity to the Hajar Mountains, Hatta is the gateway to a number of spectacular routes featured in this guide. Unusually, this particular route takes you from Hatta, through the mountains, to the Gulf of Oman. It incorporates old forts and watch-towers, scenic wadis and oases, and a hot-water spring at Ain Al Qamour.

With the development of new tarmac roads, the route has changed tremendously since the first edition of this guide appeared and more tarred roads were being constructed while this edition was being updated. It's therefore probable that more changes will affect the route. If this happens, it's advisable to leave the tar whenever possible and explore the

IN BRIEF

STARTING POINTS: Hatta or Khor Kalba.
FINISHING POINTS: Khor Kalba or Hatta.
DISTANCE: 64km or more, depending on detours.
TIME REQUIRED: One day.
CATEGORY: 4x4 recommended, but also possible in a normal saloon car.
HIGHLIGHTS: Munay, Wadi Hulw, Ohala, the hot springs at Ain Al Qamoor and the nature reserve at Khor Kalba.

many tracks leading into the wadis and up the mountains.

Of course, this applies to other routes as well – but this is all part of the excitement of off-road driving and you can use these routes as a basis for many interesting detours. Having a GPS will certainly help you with your navigation and rejoining the routes described in this guide.

How to get there

Hatta makes a better starting point since the route is clearer and easier to pinpoint than the one which begins from Kalba. The route starts at the Hatta Fort Hotel Roundabout, where you should zero your odometer (0km/N24°49.124' E56°08.056').

The mangroves at Khor Kalba Nature Reserve are a prime birding spot.

The renovated fort in the village of Ohala, overlooking Wadi Hulw.

OFF-ROAD IN THE EMIRATES

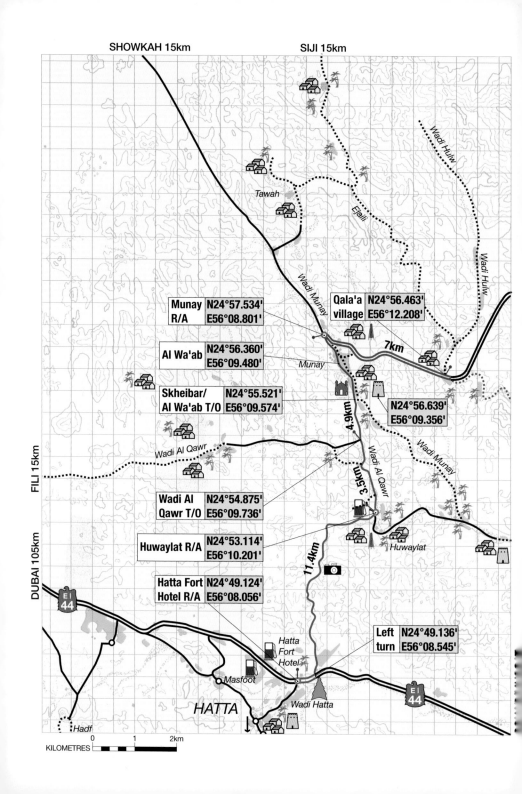

SHOWKAH 15km

SIJI 15km

Wadi Hulw

Tawah

Ejalli

Wadi Munay

Wadi Huw

Munay
R/A | N24°57.534'
E56°08.801'

Qala'a
village | N24°56.463'
E56°12.208'

7km

Al Wa'ab | N24°56.360'
E56°09.480'

Munay

Skheibar/
Al Wa'ab T/O | N24°55.521'
E56°09.574'

4.9km

N24°56.639'
E56°09.356'

FILI 15km

Wadi Al Qawr

Wadi Al Qawr

Wadi Munay

Wadi Al
Qawr T/O | N24°54.875'
E56°09.736'

3.5km

DUBAI 105km

Huwaylat R/A | N24°53.114'
E56°10.201'

Huwaylat

11.4km

Hatta Fort
Hotel R/A | N24°49.124'
E56°08.056'

E 44

Left
turn | N24°49.136'
E56°08.545'

Hatta
Fort
Hotel

E I 44

Masfoot

HATTA

Wadi Hatta

Hadf

0   1   2km

KILOMETRES

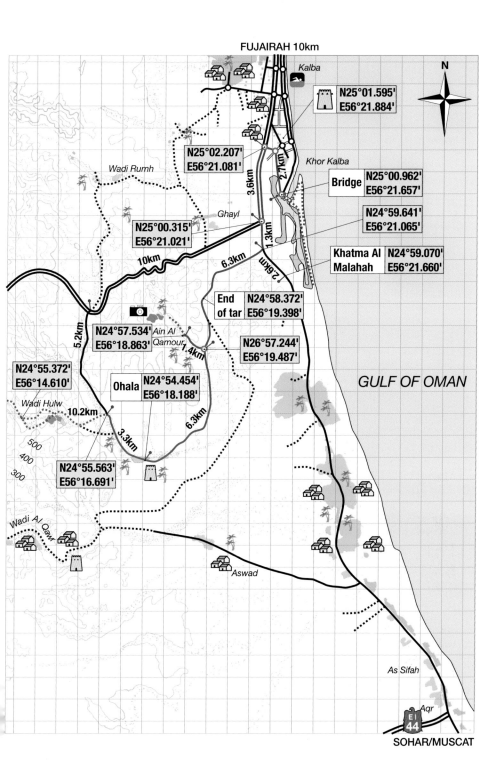

FUJAIRAH 10km

Kalba

N25°01.595'
E56°21.884'

N

N25°02.207'
E56°21.081'

Wadi Rumh

Khor Kalba

2.7km

3.6km

Bridge
N25°00.962'
E56°21.657'

N24°59.641'
E56°21.065'

Ghayl

N25°00.315'
E56°21.021'

1.3km

2.6km

Khatma Al
Malahah
N24°59.070'
E56°21.660'

10km

6.3km

End
of tar
N24°58.372'
E56°19.398'

5.2km

N24°57.534'
E56°18.863'

Ain Al
Qamour

1.4km

N26°57.244'
E56°19.487'

GULF OF OMAN

N24°55.372'
E56°14.610'

Ohala
N24°54.454'
E56°18.188'

Wadi Hulw

10.2km

3.3km

6.3km

500

400

300

N24°55.563'
E56°16.691'

Wadi Al Qawr

Aswad

As Sifah

E1
44
Aqr

SOHAR/MUSCAT

Take the dual carriageway E44 towards Oman. After 1km (1km/N24°49.136' E56°08.545'), turn north on to the single carriageway that cuts through the rugged mountains, where you'll find the scenery is absolutely magnificent.

At Huwaylat Roundabout (11.4km/ N24°53.114' E56°10.201') take the exit leading north, signposted 'Ras Al Khaimah/Masafi/Al Fojairah' (Fujairah). This road proceeds to several other interesting destinations, including Siji and Al Dhaid. At 14.9km ignore the turn-off to the left on to the tarmac road that passes through Wadi Al Qwar (N24°54.875' E56°09.736') and continue in a northerly direction towards Munay.

A little more than 1km further along the route take the turn-off to the right on to a tarmac road signposted 'Skheibar/Al Wa'ab' (16.2km/N24°55.521' E56°09.574'). Ignore the next turn-off to the right (to Skheibar) 300m further on, overlooked by an old watch-tower, and continue straight towards the village of Al Wa'ab (17.7km/N24°56.360' E56°09.480'), situated on the hilltop.

Munay

During the next kilometre Al Wa'ab merges into Munay, where you'll see a large girl's school on your right. Munay is a beautiful oasis rich in natural resources. The fort and watch-tower on the hill (N24°56.639' E56°09.356') provide a glimpse of the region's history and culture, while the gardens and palm plantations along the wadi offer good picnic spots and resting places – in fact, you can choose between driving in the wadi or on tar through the village.

Having passed through Munay, you'll reach a T-junction with the Huwaylat–Siji main road (19.8km/N24°57.168' E56°08.848'), where you turn right and travel 100m before you take another right-hand turn-off. The next landmark is a large roundabout (N24°57.534' E56°08.801') where you should take the first right on to a new dual carriageway that passes through rugged landscape *en route* to Wadi Hulw.

Wadi Hulw

The dual carriageway soon reaches the newly-constructed village of Qala'a overlooking the wadi. The name means 'fort' and it's designed in the form of local forts – a style that seems to be proving popular in the region but may be an eyesore to some visitors. At the time of writing (2002) the road terminated at the village (26.8km/N24°56.463' E56°12.208') and the old wadi road began. It probably won't be too long before the pace of development marches on and the whole route is tarred.

Wadi Hulw is picturesque, with ruins of old settlements, graves, terrace farms and the occasional pool in the wet season. However, it's also become much drier in recent years and a number of shrubs and trees in the wadi are dying.

Although the main track moves up out of the wadi (at 32.9km/N24°55.372' E56°14.610'), stay in the wadi until the track running through it joins a gravel road – where the wadi widens – and then leaves the wadi (at 36.8km). Some 200m further on turn right at a T-junction (37km/N24°55.563' E56°16.691').

North takes you directly to Khor Kalba and southeast to Ohala and Ain Al Qamour. If you're pressed for time, you should turn left (north) and take the tarmac road to Khor Kalba and Fujairah but our route proceeds towards Wahla.

Ohala and Ain Al Qamour

Ohala (40.3km) is an old oasis with a long history, as indicated by the fort

Clear water at the source of the hot-water spring at Ain Al Qamour.

(N24°54.454' E56°18.188') in the village. There are also the remains of tombs in the ground behind the fort. A drive down to the wadi will produce several oases and the village's main water source.

From Ohala the road rejoins the tarmac road and turns northeastwards and then directly north to a roundabout (46.6km/N26°57.244' E56°19.487'). The hot-water spring at Ain Al Qamour is 1.4km to the west of this roundabout.

The hot-water spring

Dense vegetation shows you are close to the hot-water spring. Drive as close as you can to the structure towards the end of the area, which is used to shade the pool below it. Park your car under one of the trees and walk towards the pool. Please note that if you see local women taking a bath you should not approach but wait until they are finished.

You can also walk the short distance upstream to visit the source of the hot spring. Taking a dip here is not recommended because the water is too hot. The temperature of the water at the pool further down is bearable since it's already travelled some distance from the source and will have cooled down. A swim is refreshing and the locals claim it has positive medical effects.

After a detour to the hot-water spring you can drive up or down the wadi in which it's situated (where you'll note the ruins of old settlements) before driving back to the roundabout.

The road to Khor Kalba

From the roundabout (49.4km) follow the sign to Fujairah and, 6.5km further on, the road joins the main coastal road (55.7km),

There's always something to see along the East Coast and good swimming too.

KHOR KALBA NATURE RESERVE

Khor Kalba Nature Reserve is located along the shores of the Gulf of Oman in the UAE just before the border with Oman. The reserve is connected to a suburb of the town of Kaliba in the emirate of Sharjah by a single bridge. It's home to scores of rare birds, fishes and a great variety of plant life.

This charming and ecologically sensitive reserve is one of the largest mangrove-dominated landscapes in all the Emirates. More than 20 endangered bird species have been spotted here, with kingfisher being the most important. More than 50 pairs of White-collared Kingfisher, the UAE's only resident kingfisher, have been counted in an area of ancient mangroves, breeding and feeding on the crabs living on the shores of the muddy creek.

Another important bird species at Khor Kalba is the migratory Blue-cheeked Bee-eater which can be seen here from March to September.

Khor Kalba is also rich in small fishes which makes it the ideal environment for visiting waders, and both blue and white phases of the Reef Heron can be found all year round.

---

where you turn left towards Khor Kalba. If you turn right here, and travel 2km, you'll reach the Omani border post of Khatam Al Malaha, where passports and visas – if applicable – are required.

Continuing left you reach a series of roundabouts: continue straight at the first one (57km/N25°00.315' E56°21.021'), right at the second (60.6km/N25°02.207' E56°21.081), right at the third (61.1km/N25°02.180' E56°21.337') – you'll now be driving parallel to the coast towards the *Khor* (creek) – and continue straight at the fourth roundabout (63.3km). Just 200m from the fourth roundabout you'll cross a bridge (N25°00.962' E56°21.657') and enter the nature reserve on the other side. This is the only access by vehicle to the area.

Khor Kalba is a scenic spot, rich in marine life with indigenous plants growing in the wetlands. The marine life, includes crabs, oysters, fish and many species of birds. There are also mangroves and marshland – where many species exist – adding to the diversity of this peaceful spot. Driving past the causeway towards the sea, you'll see ecologically-rich sand-dunes leading to flat, smooth beaches. These are scenic spots for swimming and sunbathing but make sure you don't disturb or pollute this rich nature reserve.

To return to Fujairah from Khor Kalba, drive north along the Gulf of Oman coast towards Fujairah.

The harbour at Khor Kalba, the ruins of the old fort (N25°01.595' E56°21.884'), the nearby watch-tower and the old houses are all picturesque and make good photo opportunities, while the beaches along the way offer ample private swimming spots. The distance to Fujairah is 10km.

ROUTE 12 HATTA–SIJI

This is one of the longer routes in this guide, taking you deep into the mountains in the northern UAE, where you'll see some of the country's highest villages. Even though there are several starting points for this route – Wadi Al Qawr, Maleihah/Shawkah and Siji – it would be advisable to start from Hatta on your first attempt.

How to get there

At Hatta Fort Hotel Roundabout zero your odometer (N24°49.117' E56°08.048') and follow the directions to

IN BRIEF

STARTING POINT: Hatta.
FINISHING POINT: Siji.
DISTANCE: 67km.
TIME REQUIRED: One to one-and-a-half days.
CATEGORY: 4x4.
HIGHLIGHTS: Oases and villages along Wadi Al Qawr; the old village, watch-tower and gardens at Munay; Wadi Al Ejeili's (Wadi Laili's) high-altitude villages; Najd Al Abyad Pass; scenic views at Wadi Ghabbah; Wadi Sifuni and Siji Oasis and Dam.

Huwaylat and Munay described in route 11. You may want to have a break at Munay before starting the drive to Siji.

From Munay Roundabout (21km/ N24°57.535' E56°08.802') continue in a northwesterly and northerly direction towards Siji, until the road forks (25.5km/N24°59.397' E56°07.324'). The main road continues on the left-hand side in a northwesterly direction to Siji while the right fork, signposted Wadi Al Ejeili, heads in a northeasterly direction to the same destination. Our route follows

Villagers and off-roaders enjoy the rare experience of water flowing in Wadi Siji.

the right fork and the tarmac ends at another fork (27.2km/N24°59.874' E56°08.098') where you should take the northern route up a steep hill instead of the right fork. After a further kilometre or so the oasis and village of Tawah appear (28.2km) and, after another kilometre, turn right into the wadi (29.3km/ N25°00.964' E56°07.915'). About 200m further, there's a T-junction where you have to turn left.

Beyond Wadi Tawah the track turns sharply to the east and climbs up the mountain towards Wadi Al Ejeili. After travelling just 1.7km eastwards from the point where you turned into the wadi, there's a viewpoint, at an elevation of about 500m (N25°01.211' E56°08.701'), looking over the road to Wadi Al Ejeili.

Several houses, old huts and palm groves are visible as you enter Wadi Al Ejeili (32.9km/N25°01.079' E56°09.633'). Continue to a fork where you turn right out of the wadi (36.5km/N25°02.688' E56°08.708'). A few kilometres further on there's another fork where, once again, you should keep right (40.6km/ N25°06.288' E56°07.596').

Highest villages

The drive northwards into Wadi Al Ejeili continues upstream and upwards to Najd Al Abyad Pass, reaching an elevation of 860m (42.5km). Heavy rains may wash away part of this track at times, so caution is required while driving through the area.

The villages up here are some of the UAE's highest. The mountain peak on the right of this pass rises 1,000m above sea level and is the highest point in the region. The track descends from the summit of the pass, in a northerly direction, until it reaches a fork at Wadi Ruhabah (43.6km/N25°05.744' E56°07.625').

At this fork, the track turning left (ie sharply westwards) goes to Darah and

An old fort and watch-tower are situated on a hill overlooking Munay.

Shawkah via Wadi Ruhabah, about 12km away, but our route continues northwards towards Siji. A kilometre beyond the fork (44.6km/N25°06.286' E56°07.598'), the track divides again. Turn right (eastwards) here, passing Jebel Sa'ad, until you reach the track through Wadi Hallabah.

From here, a sharp right turn eastwards takes you down a steep track to the green oasis of Sufai (46.6km/N25°06.729' E56°08.290'). The view of the village from above makes a beautiful photograph and you may even catch a glimpse of friendly villagers planting tobacco if you happen to be there at the right time (spring). Before tobacco was imported, this area used to be the main source of tobacco for neighbouring towns.

At the far end of the village there's a

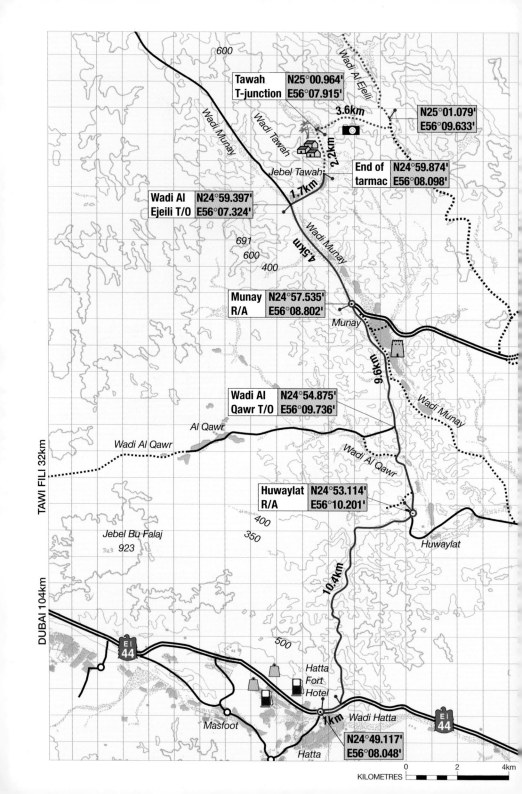

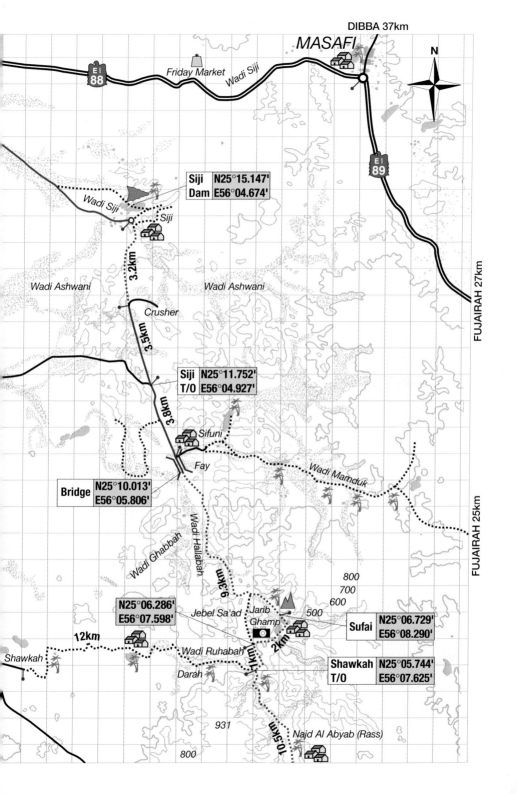

A group of off-roaders enjoy a break before the track leading into Wadi Ruhabah.

T-junction just beyond a mosque, where you should keep left. Continue in a northwesterly direction, out of Sufai, passing through several villages and wadis, including picturesque Wadi Ghababah, a short distance to the left. The track reaches a tarmac road (at 55.9km/N25°10.013' E56°05.806') just before the bridge crossing Wadi Sifuni.

There's quite a lot to explore around this area (several oases, dams, villages and Wadi Sifuni itself). However, if you don't have time, and want to complete the route quickly, continue directly to Siji.

Wadi Sifuni

After starting from the bridge at Wadi Sifuni, the two dams nearby are worth visiting, while a drive east to the source of Wadi Sifuni takes you through many oases. To get there, drive north after crossing the bridge and turn right into the new village of Sifuni. From here, drive eastwards past several villages and oases. This track continues to Wadi Mamduk (about 10km from the bridge), Farfar and Fujairah, and is described in *Off-Road in the Emirates 2*.

How to get to Siji

Cross the bridge and continue northwards until you reach a turn-off to the right signposted 'Wadi Isfini Crushers' (59.7km/N25°11.752' E56°04.927'). After 3.5km, this tarmac road veers to the right. At this point keep straight – on to a gravel road (63.1km/N25°13.500' E56°04.933') that winds round mountainous terrain before crossing Wadi Ashwani (64.8km/N25°14.243' E56°04.665'). A little more than a kilometre beyond the wadi crossing a

Healthy tobacco plants growing in the verdant oasis of Sufai.

turn-off to the right leads to Siji village.
A drive around Siji is interesting. Visit the old dam (N25°15.147' E56°04.674') and numerous oases lined up along the wadi. The 10-km drive northeast from Siji on a tarmac road will take you to the Masafi–Al Dhaid Road.

If you don't turn into Siji from Sifuni, keep straight and you'll reach the Siji Roundabout after 400m (66.4km/ N25°14.968' E56°04.420').

SHELTER

Mountain dwellers usually have separate summer and winter living quarters, which vary in their layout and building materials. Summer quarters are located at a higher elevation to catch any prevailing winds. The dwellings are more spread out and the rooms are more open to allow air inside. In contrast, winter houses are placed closer to each other and are built with denser, more solid material.

A visitor may make the mistake of thinking that a village lies abandoned whereas it's really been left only for a few months: locked or unlocked, the integrity of these homes should always be respected. There have been rare cases of campers attempting to break into houses and even taking away some of the villagers' belongings, incorrectly thinking they're no longer used or wanted. Property should always be left as it's found in these villages.

With its streams of clear water meandering through shady palm plantations and its rugged mountain scenery and rough track, the route through Tayyibah, Wadi Asimah and Wadi Ama can be quite an adventurous and exciting place to visit.

This short route lies off the Masafi–Dibba Road. The wadis were once the main route between Masafi and Dibba and you can still catch glimpses of the original tarmac along the way. The road was abandoned when the new highway was built and has gradually slipped into a state of disrepair. Nowadays, the track is rough in many parts and, in places, requires careful negotiation over boulders and rocks moved by seasonal flooding.

Although the route is off the beaten track and the going tough, it's well worth

IN BRIEF

STARTING POINT: Masafi.
FINISHING POINT: Dibba.
DISTANCE: A 14km detour off the main road.
TIME: Half a day or less.
CATEGORY: Rough, 4x4 only.
HIGHLIGHTS: The village and oasis of Tayyibah, the oasis of Asimah, some spectacular mountain scenery, palm plantations, streams and three great wadis: Wadi Ghali Abadilah, Wadi Ama and Wadi Al Uyaynah.

the effort because of the breathtaking mountain scenery. And each time you travel through this area, it seems to look different. . . .

How to get there

There are several ways of approaching this route, but the best and simplest is to start from Masafi, where you should zero your odometer at the Masafi Roundabout (N25°17.976' E56°10.017'). Take the Masafi–Dibba Road, signposted 'Tayyibah 8km, Dibba 37km' and head north from the roundabout. After a couple of kilometres you'll pass the Masafi mineral-water bottling factory. Continue for another kilometre or so and you'll pass the entrance to the old village of Masafi on the left-hand side (3.3km). A visit to this village makes a short but interesting excursion.

The next landmark, a communication tower on the right (9.8km), indicates

A group of villagers enjoy a pleasant winter's afternoon in old Tayyibah.

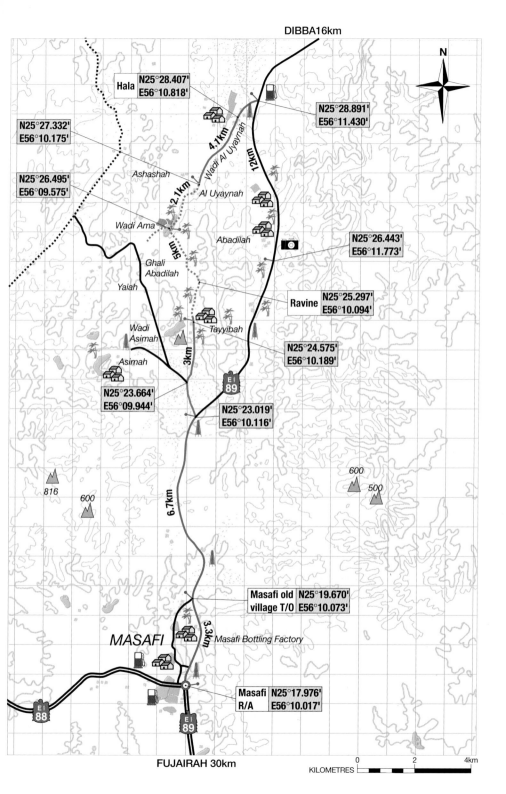

DIBBA 16km

N

Hala N25°28.407'
E56°10.818'

N25°28.891'
E56°11.430'

N25°27.332'
E56°10.175'

4.1km

Wadi Al Uyaynah

12km

N25°26.495'
E56°09.575'

Ashashah

2.1km

Al Uyaynah

5km

Wadi Ama

Abadilah

N25°26.443'
E56°11.773'

Ghali
Abadilah

Yalah

Ravine N25°25.297'
E56°10.094'

Wadi
Asimah

Tayyibah

N25°24.575'
E56°10.189'

3km

Asimah

E l
89

N25°23.664'
E56°09.944'

N25°23.019'
E56°10.116'

600

816

600

500

6.7km

Masafi old N25°19.670'
village T/O E56°10.073'

MASAFI

3.3km

Masafi Bottling Factory

E l
88

E l
89

Masafi N25°17.976'
R/A E56°10.017'

FUJAIRAH 30km

KILOMETRES 0   2   4km

ANIMALS OF THE DESERT

The desert areas of the Emirates provide evidence of a surprising wealth of animal life, although it's likely you'll see only a small proportion of the animals. While there's an interesting diversity of species, the numbers within each species are generally small. Also, many are nocturnal, hiding during the day in caves, in the sand and beneath stones, and are therefore seldom seen.

Ruppell's sand fox

Foxes may be seen in the mountains and even near urban settlements. Among the smaller mammals that inhabit the sandy desert, gerbils, and in particular three-toed gerbils, are noteworthy. They are nocturnal and their tracks can be observed in the sand in the early morning, possibly along with the tracks of the predatory sand cat, now rare. Still relatively common in nearly all environments are hares and the Ethiopian and Brandt's hedgehog.

Animals in the desert have adapted to a harsh environment of high temperatures and very little water–and avoid extreme conditions–by making various anatomical adjustments. They use water incredibly sparingly and get their moisture requirements by licking at early-morning dew, from the blood of their prey or by eating desert-plant foods with a high water content.

Some species, including mammals such as the jerboa, are able to obtain sufficient moisture through their food. Other species are able to survive dry periods in stages of latent life. Some butterflies, for example, may wait for several years as pupae for the next rain, while small freshwater crabs, whose eggs remain in hard cysts for years, appear fully-grown in small puddles of water a few days after rain has fallen.

you're approaching the access road to Tayyibah. A left turn in a northeasterly direction (10km/N25°23.019' E56°10.116') takes you to another left turn (at 11.3km/N25°23.664' E56°09.944'). This leads to the village of Asimah but our route continues straight to the village of Tayyibah. (However, if you do drive to Asimah, you'll find another beautiful oasis, well worth a visit.)

The track through the wadi begins in Tayyibah (13km/N25°24.575' E56°10.189') where you can park your 4x4 and walk round the village. Keep on the main track through the village – ie the old tarmac road that appears and disappears – and take the central track at the triple fork. A sharp right turn then

leads straight into the oasis.

At 13.9km turn left into a tributary of the wadi, drive to a fork that leads up out of the wadi into the old village, turn right and you'll arrive at the old mosque. From here there's a great view of the whole area, especially the oasis. The vegetation is profuse, with lots of fruit trees such as mango, orange, grapefruit and lemon.

The wadi

After exploring the old village of Tayyibah, return to the main wadi (15km/ N25°24.938' E56°10.010') and continue downstream in a northerly direction. Wadi

Wadi Ghali Abadilah is surrounded by mountains and is strictly a 4x4 route.

Ghali Abadilah is surrounded by rocky mountains with water flowing in the *falaj*, palms and lush gardens (15.3km/ N25°25.089' E56°10.089'). Unlike today, this was once a popular road frequented by a stream of cars. Nowadays, the route that leads to Wadi Al Uyaynah is difficult to traverse. In some places, you may even need one of your passengers to guide you over or between rocks and boulders.

Your progress may be impeded if there's been a flash flood in the area shortly before your trip. However, since the villagers need to keep the track open, it might just be usable. Driving down the wadi is quite a pleasant journey. The passage is narrow and terraced gardens keep cropping up and disappearing along the way.

You'll find clear water and a canopy of shade in the verdant Wadi Al Uyaynah.

Wadi Al Uyaynah

Wadi Al Uyaynah, at a point where three wadis converge (19km/N25°26.495' E56°09.575'), may be only 5km from Tayyibah but it could feel as though you've been driving for hours. However, you'll be well rewarded for your efforts once you reach your destination. Crystal-clear water cascades through this verdant oasis almost all year round and the wadi is full of trees that form a canopy of shade. Leave your 4x4 at the beginning of the wadi and trek upstream into Wadi Ama – a 300–500-m climb will produce many scenic picnic spots with clear water pools.

Once you've explored Wadi Ama and the oases along Wadi Al Uyaynah, continue downstream. The wadi slowly turns drier and rockier until you reach the tarmac road (21.1km/N25°27.332' E56°10.175'). This road passes the village of Hala (23.7km/N25°28.407' E56°10.818') before the junction with the Masafi–Dibba Road (25.2km/N25°28.891' E56°11.430'). Driving in a northeasterly direction from here takes you to Dibba (at 40km) and in a southerly direction back to Masafi Roundabout.

Enjoying a break in the oasis where the three wadis in this route converge.

A colourful door in typical rural style takes shape in the village of Hala.

ROUTE 14 WADI WURAYYAH WATERFALL

Wadi Wurayyah is located deep within the Hajar Mountains, near the East Coast of the UAE. The scenic route is fairly straightforward and the cool waterfall and pools at the end of the drive will reward your efforts.

This is a good outing for people living or spending a weekend on the East Coast although it's best done during the week, when it's less crowded and even more enjoyable.

How to get there

At the roundabout near the entrance to the Oceanic Hotel, near Khor Fakkan Bay in Khor Fakkan, zero your odometer

IN BRIEF

STARTING POINT: Khor Fakkan.
FINISHING POINT: Wadi Wurayyah Waterfall.
DISTANCE: 21.4km (one way).
TIME REQUIRED: Half a day to a full day.
CATEGORY: Possible in a normal car although you'll have to clamber up and down a hill to the waterfall.
HIGHLIGHTS: Several pools, waterfalls and a beautiful drive through Wadi Wurayyah.

(N25°22.359' E56°20.852').
Drive northwards towards Dibba, crossing three sets of roundabouts (at 2.2, 3.2 and 4km). After travelling 1.1km beyond the third roundabout do a U-turn and go back 700m before taking a tarmac road to your right (at 5.8km/N25°24.715' E56°20.989'), that runs away from the coast towards the mountains in a southwesterly direction.

Initially the road is straight but it veers westwards after a few kilometres and passes a turn-off to a dam and a water-bottling plant (at 10.7km/N25°23.344' E56°18.655'). Don't take this turn-off but continue straight in a westerly direction to a fork at 11.8km, where you should

The track leading to Wadi Wurayyah Waterfall is covered with small rocks.

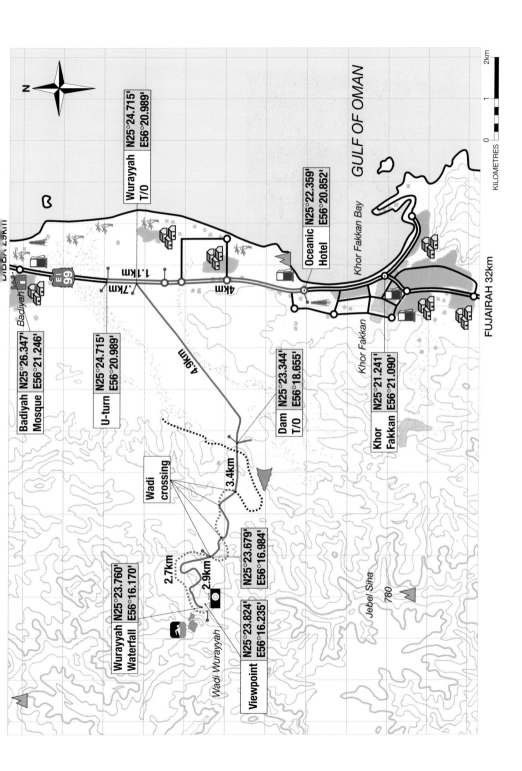

N

GULF OF OMAN

DIBBA 29km

E 99

Badiyah

Khor Fakkan Bay

Khor Fakkan

Jebel Siha

780

Wadi Wurayyah

FUJAIRAH 32km

Wurayyah
T/O
N25°24.715'
E56°20.989'

Oceanic
Hotel
N25°22.359'
E56°20.852'

Badiyah
Mosque
N25°26.347'
E56°21.246'

U-turn
N25°24.715'
E56°20.989'

Dam
T/O
N25°23.344'
E56°18.655'

Khor
Fakkan
N25°21.241'
E56°21.090'

Wadi
crossing

Wurayyah
Waterfall
N25°23.760'
E56°16.170'

N25°23.679'
E56°16.984'

Viewpoint
N25°23.824'
E56°16.235'

1.1km

.7km

4km

4.9km

3.4km

2.7km

2.9km

0   1   2km

KILOMETRES

Off-roaders enjoy a relaxing moment next to the stream above the falls.

keep to the right. This is a quiet and pleasant road on which to drive and in several spots crosses Wadi Wurayyah with its steep, vertical walls. As wadi crossings can be dangerous in flash floods, you should always proceed with caution.

At the fourth wadi crossing (14.1km/ N25°23.679' E56°16.984'), you can either keep to the left on the tarmac road or turn right onto a wadi track going directly

north. Because of the rough and rocky nature of the track along the wadi bed, the former route is recommended.

Continue to the upper level, from where you get a bird's-eye view of the falls, the pool and the landscape surrounding them (17km/25°23.824' E56°16.235')

A camera here is a must and you should also keep your eye on any children since there are no guard rails and the loose gravel can be quite slippery. From here you can either clamber down to the waterfall or drive back to the wadi entrance point and make a sharp left turn into the wadi (18.7km).

The track to the waterfall

The track across the rocks and boulders to the waterfall is 2.7km long. You won't be able to exceed 10–20 km/h here, so it will take a little while to reach your destination (at 21.4km/N25°23.760' E56°16.170') even in a sturdy 4x4.

You'll come across several pools before you reach the falls. As you get closer to the waterfall you'll see more plants, especially bamboo shoots and wild oleanders, indicating an abundance of water. The landscape is spectacular with the mountain slopes cloaked in rocks and gravel of autumnal shades and harsh boulders on either side of the wadi.

The waterfall

Although you can hear the tumbling water from some distance, it's not enough to prepare you for the sheer immensity with which it hits you as you near the waterfall. The actual waterfall is seven to eight metres high, but the rapids are double this height. The waterfall flows all year round but the amount of water varies depending on the season and the amount of rain during the year.

The clear pool at the base of the waterfall is a delightful place for a refreshing swim

REPTILES

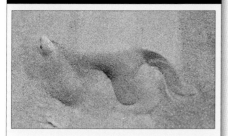

As in many other arid areas, reptiles in the UAE are represented by numerous different species. They are well suited to the climatic conditions in that they need very little water, are cold-blooded and don't require food as often as mammals.

Some groups such as the skinks have adjusted particularly well. The Arabian sand skink and Wiegmann's skink, for instance, can 'swim' in moving sand. Another species, the ocellated skink, is also found.

A number of snake species inhabit the desert but mostly you see only their tracks. Relatively common are the poisonous sand viper, the equally poisonous common carpet viper and Burton's carpet viper – wadis being a preferred habitat of the latter two.

Also found in wadis as well as oasis gardens are several non-poisonous snake species such as the cliff racer, hunting for toads and other small animals to eat.

The geckos, all of which are nocturnal, occur in nearly all environments. The fan-footed gecko and Gallagher's gecko prefer rocky areas, while other species live on the gravel plains. Many species of the genera Hemidactylus, Phyllodactylus and Ptyodactylus have adhesive toes and belong to the group of climbing geckos which also occur in human settlements.

Among the lacertid lizards, some common species worth mentioning are the widespread Arabian spinyfoot, the Sinai agama and an edible lizard, the spiny-tailed lizard. The largest Arabian reptile is the grey monitor, which can grow up to 1,2 metres in length. A permanently active hunter, it lives in the marginal areas of the Rub al Khali.

The waterfall gushes into a beautiful pool, desecrated by graffiti.

(and another where you'll feel the nips of tiny fish). Sadly, however, the beauty of this spot has been spoilt by graffiti.

A climb above the waterfall will take you to a plateau from where you can see the stream above it and there's a very pleasant walk along the wadi and the stream beyond this point. The waterfall is very popular with picnickers and it's best to avoid the crowd by going there on weekdays.

ROUTE 15 DIBBA TO RAS AL KHAIMAH

Located in the northernmost part of the UAE and in the southernmost part of Oman's Musandam, this route incorporates some of the highest plateaux and peaks of the Arabian Peninsula. The area is called Ruus Al Jibal, and is accessible from Dibba and Ras Al Khaimah. Access, however, is easier from Dibba and, in the case of a morning departure, it's better to travel this way as the sun will be behind you. Because of the higher altitudes, this is one of the better routes for the summer

IN BRIEF

STARTING POINTS: Dibba or Ras Al Khaimah.
FINISHING POINTS: Ras Al Khaimah or Dibba.
DISTANCE: 88km, excluding any detours.
TIME REQUIRED: One day.
CATEGORY: Mountainous, steep and windy track; rough after a flash flood. A 4x4 is therefore recommended.
HIGHLIGHTS: Old stone houses, mountain villages and terraced fields, panoramic views with high peaks and plateaux, detours to the coast. Suitable as a summer drive.

months. The route incorporates two spectacular wadis: Wadi Khab A'Shamis and Wadi Bih.

How to get there from Dibba

The easier, more frequently used access to these two wadis is from Dibba. Zero your odometer at the Mahlab Roundabout on the Masafi–Dibba Road at Dibba Ghurfah (0km/ E25°35.812', E56°16.696'). This roundabout, which is decorated with dolphins, is situated 37km from Masafi, 35km from Khor Fakkan and

The start of the pass between Wadi Khab A'Shamis and Wadi Bih. This section of the route takes you to a high plateau dotted with traditional settlements.

Badiyah Mosque near Dibba (the starting point of this route) is the oldest mosque in the Emirates and is thought to date back some 1,400 years.

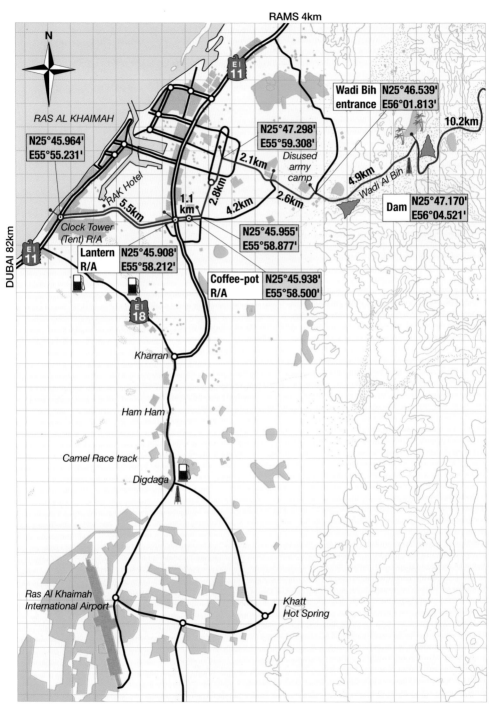

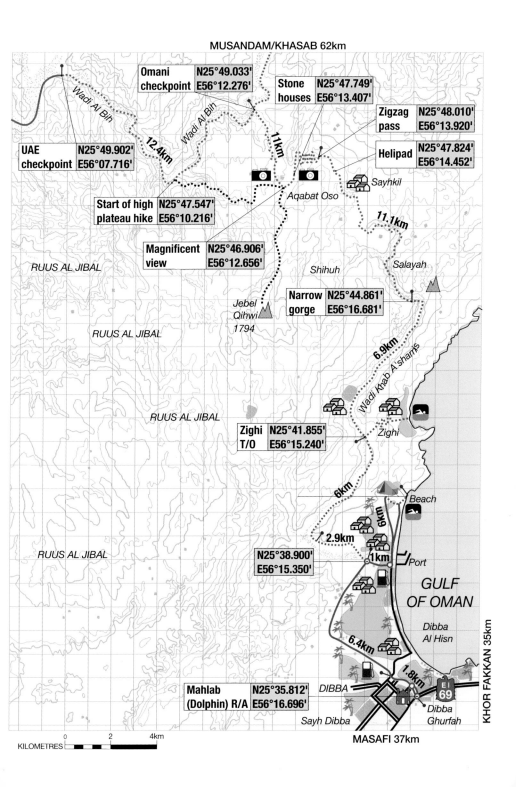

MUSANDAM/KHASAB 62km

Omani checkpoint | N25°49.033' E56°12.276'

Stone houses | N25°47.749' E56°13.407'

Zigzag pass | N25°48.010' E56°13.920'

Helipad | N25°47.824' E56°14.452'

UAE checkpoint | N25°49.902' E56°07.716'

Wadi Al Bih

12.4km

11km

Sayhkil

Aqabat Oso

Start of high plateau hike | N25°47.547' E56°10.216'

Magnificent view | N25°46.906' E56°12.656'

RUUS AL JIBAL

Shihuh

Salayah

11.1km

Jebel Qihwi 1794

Narrow gorge | N25°44.861' E56°16.681'

RUUS AL JIBAL

6.9km

Wadi Khab A'shams

RUUS AL JIBAL

Zighi T/O | N25°41.855' E56°15.240'

Zighi

6km

Beach

6km

2.9km

1km | Port

N25°38.900' E56°15.350'

RUUS AL JIBAL

GULF OF OMAN

Dibba Al Hisn

6.4km

1.8km

E 69

Mahlab (Dolphin) R/A | N25°35.812' E56°16.696'

DIBBA

Dibba Ghurfah

Sayh Dibba

MASAFI 37km

KHOR FAKKAN 35km

KILOMETRES

0   2   4km

The beach beyond Dibba Port makes a pleasant picnic or overnight camping spot.

60km from Fujairah, 20m above sea level.

Drive northwest into the centre of Dibba and cross one roundabout and two junctions. Keep on this road. After 1.8km you'll pass a sign saying 'Welcome to Oman' and just beyond that there's a petrol station where you can top up with fuel. Further on there's a roundabout (8.2km/N25°38.900' E56°15.350') where a right turn takes you eastwards towards the sea and a left turn leads you towards the mountains.

At this point you'll need to choose whether to head directly towards the mountains or take a short side trip to the coast near Dibba (there's an alternative detour to the coast slightly further on). However, as long as you can get back to the roundabout before noon, you can make it to Ras Al Khaimah by sunset.

To the beach
If you have the time, the 12-km round trip to the beach is a must. To get to the best part of the beach, turn right at the roundabout and follow the sign to Nsour and Al Husayiah. Turn north after 1.5km at the roundabout towards Al Mina (Dibba Port). This road takes you through several small villages and oases until it reaches a dead-end after another 3km. From here, take the sandy track to the right and drive toward the sea at the end of the asphalt road.

Drive to the beach where the sand is compact, making driving to the water's edge easy. Situated at the northernmost end of the beach, in this most remote corner of the Omani Coast, are the ruins of two small fishing settlements. A walk through the roofless rooms of these ruins could leave you with a somewhat eerie feeling.

If you plan to camp overnight this is a good spot but make sure your tent is pitched above the high-tide line. In the evening note the green glow of the phosphorous at the water's edge, where

Wadi Khab A'Shamis boasts some of the region's most spectacular scenery.

tiny marine creatures are washed up by the waves. A morning walk over the rocky edge at the end of the beach should also prove rewarding for those who enjoy the wonders of nature.

Wadi Khab A'Shamis

Having explored the beach, and possibly a bit more of Dibba, return to the roundabout (ie to the original 8.2-km point). Make sure you've filled your petrol tank and have enough food and water for the journey. From the roundabout continue straight on a well-graded track and, after a little more than 1km (9.4km), you'll already be surrounded by the rocky mountains and the track forks. Go left here, following the sign to Khasab, until you reach a second fork where you go right, following another sign to Khasab (11.1km) on this well-signposted route.

The flat gravel track proceeds in a northerly to northeasterly direction alongside a fairly flat but boulder-strewn wadi that runs parallel to the Gulf of Oman, now hidden from sight by the imposing mountain ranges. Soon you'll reach the ruins of an old settlement built of stone – the first of many along the way (13.2km).

There are also more modern farms and numerous goats. Some villagers have built their dwellings from stone, using part of the mountainside as a wall. These dwellings are used in the winter, while the houses located on the mountaintop are more suited to the hot summers.

A newly constructed track (at 17.1km/ N25°41.855' E56°15.240') offers a rewarding but tortuous 5-km zig-zag detour to the top of the mountain and down again to the remote coastal fishing village of Zighi. The view from the top of the pass is quite spectacular and reminiscent of Oman's stunning Musandam area to the north of this route, while the beach itself is delightful. (At

the time of going to press, an earth tremor had damaged the pass and cut off vehicular access to Zighi.)

Continuing northwards for the next 10km, the track criss-crosses the wadi at several locations. Crossing the wadi at these points becomes difficult and sometimes impossible after a heavy flooding and the large boulders along the rocky wadi are a sign of frequent flash flooding. At such times the boulders are often dislocated, causing the track to become blocked or washed away. At other times, rockfalls may also create blockages. Fortunately, since the track is used regularly, it also enjoys regular maintenance.

The wadi gets narrower as you proceed until there's space for only one vehicle (24km/N25°44.861' E56°16.681'. The high vertical rocky walls of the wadi are imposing and the narrow passageway filters the midday sun, creating a unique atmosphere. There's a fork to the left (at 30.5km) that you can ignore and, after a few more kilometres, the narrow gorge opens out and passes a helipad (33.9km/N25°47.824', E56°14.452').

Continuing in the general direction of Ras Al Khaimah, the track gradually veers from north to west and the mountains start levelling off, allowing long and uninterrupted views of the distant peaks.

Zigzag pass

As you progress, the vistas of narrow gorges and high mountains slowly give way to a panoramic view of the plateau above. Less noticeable is the fact that you've slowly been gaining altitude and will already have climbed to a height of 663m at the start of the zigzag pass that takes you out of Wadi Khab A'Shamis (35.1km/N25°48.010' E56°13.920').

Low gear and careful driving up (and down) the pass are essential. The drive

ALL ABOUT WADIS

A wadi is a depression in the mountains – or in gravel plains or dune areas – caused by natural processes such as the movement of the earth's surface and weathering. Water from the surrounding areas runs into these wadis and, being the course of least resistance, they carry the water to wherever they lead, be it sea, lake or plain. In other words, wadis are watercourses – according to the Westernised version of the word. According to the literal translation from the Arabic, however, wadis are valleys.

Traditionally, wadis are a source of water for people living in rural areas, and most oases and villages have sprung up because of their proximity. Tayibbah, Asimah, Masafi, Hatta and Buraimi are some examples in this book.

Another traditional use of the wadi is as a travelling route, whether through dunes or mountains, between towns and villages, or even between countries. Wadi Al Qawr, for instance, was used as a route between the UAE and Oman, while Wadi Ham and Wadi Siji together connect Fujairah, through the mountains, to the gravel plains of the rest of the UAE.

Some wadis were originally river beds stretching to the sea. Over time, and through lack of water and flooding, some wadis – such as Wadi Al Faya – have dried, been silted up by moving sand and become disconnected from their original destination. Others, however, still flow into the sea after heavy flooding, the wadi that runs through Al Dhaid and Falaj Al Mualla being a good example here.

Some of the most scenic drives in this book are through wadis. What makes them so beautiful are the meandering tracks passing through oases, the water itself and the plants which have flourished because of the proximity of the water, especially flowering plants such as the oleander.

Of special interest here is the way people have controlled the course of the water flow by building a falaj (irrigation-channel) system into the oases, leading the water to where it's most needed. Some of these aflaj (plural of falaj) date back many hundreds of years, and their presence is the reason for the continued existence of the oases and villages today.

Another characteristic of wadis is their geological importance. Because of their continuous erosion by water, wind, sun and the movement of the earth, an area of visual pleasure and geological interest has been exposed. A variety of shapes, forms, colours and texture show the layers of rock and tell us much about the geological composition of the area.

Because a watercourse can run from mountain to plains, exposing the variety of compositions along the way, a wadi provides a continuous journey of knowledge and change. Driving through a wadi really is like taking a journey through the geological history of the earth. Take a drive through Wadi Bih, or through Wadi Sharm and Wadi Qahfi, and you'll undoubtedly agree.

There are several small settlements on the plateau between the two wadis in this route.

finally levels off on the summit, where there are several small settlements, 950m above sea level, built to catch the breeze during the hotter months.

The houses in these settlements have stone walls and wooden roofs partially covered with earth. Be careful not to trespass as most houses are not locked and their boundaries are unmarked.

A typical household here comprises small units of rooms grouped together, serving as sitting rooms, sleeping rooms, stores and animal sheds. Some of the villagers are totally self-sufficient through their agriculture and goat herding. It's a hard way of life and many of the villagers are gradually moving to the cities, causing the population to decline and the villages to become abandoned. Some of the villages on this route are Sayhkil, Salayah and

Agabat. The flat area near the first village (37km) is suitable for camping, picnicking or just unwinding after the long journey.

After another 3km the track reaches its highest point at 1,042m (39.7km), where there's a plateau with a breathtaking view of the majestic but forbidding Shihuh Mountains and the terraced villages and farmlands dotted on the mountainsides. The lines of the rock strata here have a pleasing symmetry, while the stripes of colour illustrate the influence of the forces that formed the mountains.

Wadi Bih

Having crossed the highest point of the route, the track starts a downhill descent in a steep and windy section. The descent is so radical that the elevation difference of more than 700m from the highest point to Wadi Bih takes just 5km.

During the zigzag descent, the wide mouth of the magnificent wadi appears in the distance to the north. If you happen to be here at the right time – a crisp winter's morning or late afternoon, for instance – you'll have one of the most stunning views in the whole of Arabia.

Wadi Bih is reached at an elevation of 319m (46.1km/N25°49.033' E56°12.276'). Here you'll be greeted by the Omani border guards who have fenced off the northern entrance – the way to Khasab, 62km away. Although a road permit from the Omani authorities prior to arrival should guarantee your passage further north, our route proceeds in a westerly direction.

Continue downstream along the wadi and drive to the UAE checkpoint (58.5km/N25°49.902' E56°07.716') where you'll be asked to show your identification, so have your driver's licence handy. Beyond this point there's a public telephone – and a tarmac road that runs all the way to Ras Al Khaimah has been laid out on the wadi bed. Please note that both checkpoints are in restricted areas where photography is not allowed.

The road forks immediately beyond the UAE checkpoint. Take the fork on the left and head south. During the next 8km the wadi becomes noticeably sandier. Slightly further on, if there's been rain in recent months, you should see a large body of water in the dam constructed in the wadi.

Drive round the dam (67,7km/ N25°47.170' E56°04.521') and, after another kilometre, a telecommunication tower and telephone exchange appear on the left. Take the road to the left immediately after the exchange, turning in a southwesterly direction.

At the time of going to press, there were no signposts here or on the way to Ras Al Khaimah. Although the rest of the route is described in the table below, keep it in mind that your general direction is west, towards Ras Al Khaimah, from where the highway runs (parallel to the sea) to Sharjah, Dubai and Abu Dhabi.

Route directions from Wadi Bih to the Tent Roundabout and the Ras Al Khaimah–Sharjah Road appear below.

DISTANCE	GPS	DIRECTIONS
68.8km	N25°47.555' E56°04.340'	Turn left (west) at telecom tower.
73.7km	N25°46.539' E56°01.813'	Turn left (west) at disused army camp.
78.4km	N25°47.298' E55°59.308'	Turn left (south) to Ras Al Khaimah.
79.4km	N25°46.845' E55°59.057'	Roundabout. Go straight (south).
81.2km	N25°45.955' E55°58.877'	Crossroads. Turn right (west).
81.8km	N25°45.938' E55°58.500'	Coffee-pot Roundabout. Go straight (west).
82.3km	N25°45.908' E55°58.212'	Lantern Roundabout. Go straight (west).
83.5km	N25°45.770' E55°57.431'	End of *khor* (creek). Road turns northwest.
85.6km	N25°46.086' E55°56.380'	Ras Al Khaimah Hotel. Go straight (west).
87.8km	N25°45.964' E55°55.231'	Tent Roundabout. End of trip.

At the Tent Roundabout turn left (southwest) on to the Ras Al Khaimah–Dubai Road or right (northeast) toward the Ras Al Khaimah town centre. The route back to Sharjah and Dubai is clearly signposted.

BASIC ARABIC FOR OFF-ROADERS

Here are a few useful words and phrases, written phonetically for those who cannot speak Arabic:

Basic words

Thanks	shukhran
Thank you very much	shukhran jazilan
You're welcome	afwan
Please	min fadlak (m), min fadliki (f)
I am sorry	ana asef
Yes	na'am, aywah
No	la
I do not have	ma'indee
There isn't any	mafee
How much?	bikam?
Okay, lovely, good	zain
And	wa
Also	kaman

Greetings

Greeting (Peace be upon you)	assalaam alaykum
Response (On you be peace)	wa'alaykum as salam
Good morning	sabah al khayr
Good morning in response	sabah al noor
Good evening	masa' al khayr
Good evening in response	masa' al noor
Hello	marhaba
Hello in response	marhabtayn
Welcome	ahlan wasahlan
Welcome in response	ahlan beek (m), ahlan beeky (f)
How are you?	kayf halak (m), kayf halek (f)
Fine thank you	bikhayr shukhran
Please join us	tafaddal ma'ana
Goodbye	ma'assalama

Introductions

My name is . . .	ismee . . .
What is your name?	shoo ismak (m), shoo ismek (f)
Where are you from?	inta min ayy balad?
I am from . . .	ana min . . .
Africa	Afriqiah
America	Amreekah
Australia	Ostrāliah
Britain	Bareetania
Europe	Awropah
India	Alhind

Directions

Is this the road to . . .	hal hadah huwa al tareeq ila . . .
How far is the road?	kam masafat al tareeq
Can you point the way to . . .	mumkin tadullinee ala. . .
What is the name of this village?	shoo ism hadee al qariayh?
Where can I buy petrol?	min wain ashtari betrol?
Left	yasar
Right	yameen
Straight	seedah

Questions

May we camp here?	mumken nukhayyem hinah?
How many/much?	kam?
Where?	wayn?
When?	mata?
Which?	ayy?
What?	shoo?
Why?	laysh?
Who?	meen?
How?	kayf?
To/for	ila
In/at	fee
From	min

Numbers

Zero	sifr
One	wahed
Two	ithnain
Three	thalathah
Four	arba'ah
Five	khamsah
Six	sittah
Seven	saba'a
Eight	thamaniyah
Nine	tis a'ah
10	asharah
20	ishreen
30	talatheen
40	arba'een
50	khamseen
60	sitteen
70	sabe'en
80	thamaneen
90	tise'en
100	miyyah
1000	alf

Acknowledgements

One of the best ways of enjoying the wadis and desert regions of the Emirates is with friends and loved ones, and I'd like to thank the Almighty for creating such a beautiful and varied world of sea, desert, mountains and wadis, and for the fresh water that brings life to this barren land, creating oases to add to the beauty.

My gratitude goes to the leaders of the United Arab Emirates for enabling us all to travel so freely into the interior of the country, to explore, enjoy, relax and record our experiences.

Land Rover, without whom publication of this book would not have been possible, have my appreciation. I'd specially like to thank Ashley Masefield, Matthew McClurg and Nicola Frudd for their support and for arranging vehicles to be photographed, and Al Tayer Motors for trusting me with their vehicles.

The villagers who, through their continuous efforts, have kept the natural beauty, heritage and culture alive in the remote corners of the UAE, also deserve a mention. Their hospitality and generosity have always amazed me, and I have not found any other people as helpful when it comes to giving a hand in emergencies.

I am enormously indebted to my family for their continuous encouragement. My mom has been a tremendous support while my sister Ghazal and her sons Raed and Shahab, and my son Arash, have been company on some of the trips and given a hand in preparations and taking notes.

I'd like to thank Motivate Publishing, especially Ian Fairservice for his dedication in producing books on the UAE, its history, traditions and nature.

I'd also like to thank David Steele, the senior editor of Motivate's books department, who was very generous with his time. To make sure the information was as accurate and user-friendly as possible, David retravelled most of the routes before editing them, and provided some of his photos for the book.

My thanks to Jackie Nel for her continuous encouragement and all her help in editing the book and maps.

Thanks, too, to Johnson Machado and Fred Dittlau for their design work and never-ending maps, and to Alison Ashbee, Zelda Pinto and Simon O'Herlihy, also from Motivate.

Again, Asha Bhatia earns my thanks for providing the spark that originally started this series of books.

Coleman and their distributors, Picnico, provided the whole range of their outdoor equipment, which brought me comfort off-road. Garmin supplied two GPS receivers – a most useful device which helped to improve my maps and brought security to my trips to the unknown.

In addition, I'd like to mention Cyril Pinto and Suchitra Chaudhary of *Gulf News*, Morteza and Maryam Farzana and their girls, Hassan Tavakoli and his family, Bhaskar Bino and Malihah Sobati, Pam and Toby Morley, Jill Spruce, Gordon and Marjolein Rouquette, Farah Abolghasemi, Shahram and Faranak Azizi and the rest of Farayand, Mina and Hassan Roshan and their children, and Kathy Hyde and the rest of the American BC camp-out.

Thanks also go to Siamak Zandi, Vinod and Bhupesh Suthar, Tazegol, Farid Ben Driss, James Koshy, Nicolas Hamawi, Khalig Ahmed, Roen Menazes, David Waring, Emad Salaheddin, Ahmed Al Falasi, Alexander, Nasser Hasanain, Shabbir Dawoodi and Farid Semaan.

Finally, I'd like to express my appreciation to the late Ronald Codrai for sharing his experiences of 50 years ago when he travelled many of the same routes. His beautiful photographs are still an inspiration and an education.

About the Author

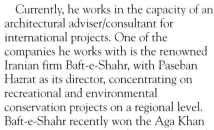

For as long as he can remember, Dariush Zandi has been attracted to out-of-the-way places. As a child he loved nothing better than to leave his native Teheran and travel to the villages. "Life there intrigued me with its simplicity," he recalls.

His university years in the United States gave him ample opportunity to experience the great outdoors and, when he graduated as an architect, he joined a Manhattan/Soho firm, Claude Samton & Associates, which specialises in designing houses, parks and recreation areas. He still keeps in touch with the principle of this firm, Claude, and visits his former colleagues regularly.

After this, Dariush worked with Jafar Tukan Architects in Amman, Jordan, before returning to the US to continue his studies.

He completed his master's degree in urban-design architecture and town planning and, after further international travels, joined Dubai Municipality, where he was Senior Architect and Town Planner from 1981 to 1994. His work involved town planning, parks and recreation projects; he was also project co-ordinator for several major projects, including the Dubai master plan and the restoration of Sheikh Saeed's House (the former residence of Dubai's ruling Al Maktoum family) and Hatta Heritage Village.

Currently, he works in the capacity of an architectural adviser/consultant for international projects. One of the companies he works with is the renowned Iranian firm Baft-e-Shahr, with Paseban Hazrat as its director, concentrating on recreational and environmental conservation projects on a regional level. Baft-e-Shahr recently won the Aga Khan Architectural Award.

He also runs an art gallery, Total Arts, at The Courtyard, a complex designed and built by him. The gallery specialises in traditional and Middle Eastern arts and crafts and aims to discover and expose new artists, as well as enrich the cultural heritage of the UAE.

Dariush is an avid collector of Middle Eastern arts and crafts himself, and has made his collection available for viewing in the gallery, with the long-term goal of turning it into a Museum of Middle Eastern Art.

Through the Iranian Business Council, of which he's an active member, he keeps in close contact with the community.

In addition, Dariush is a professional photographer and his photographs have appeared in many books and magazines. He is the author of a second volume of *Off-Road in the Emirates* and co-author of *Architectural Heritage of the Gulf*, also published by Motivate. He is currently working on revising and updating *Off-Road 2*.

THE ARABIAN HERITAGE SERIES

NATURAL HISTORY AND CULTURE

Birds of the Southern Gulf
Dave Robinson and Adrian Chapman

Falconry and Birds of Prey in the Gulf
David Remple and Christian Gross

Seashells of Eastern Arabia
S Peter Dance

Sketchbook Arabia
Margaret Henderson

The Living Seas
Frances Dipper and Tony Woodward

The Oasis Al Ain Memoirs of 'Doctora Latifa'
Gertrude Dyck

UAE GUIDES

A Portrait of Ras Al Khaimah
Shirley Kay

Abu Dhabi Garden City of the Gulf
Peter Hellyer and Ian Fairservice

Al Ain – Oasis City
Peter Hellyer and Rosalind Buckton

Dubai Gateway to the Gulf
Edited by Ian Fairservice

Fujairah An Arabian Jewel
Peter Hellyer

Sharjah Heritage and Progress
Shirley Kay

COUNTRY GUIDES

Enchanting Oman
Shirley Kay

Kuwait A New Beginning
Gail Seery

Land of the Emirates
Shirley Kay

Saudi Arabia Profile of a Kingdom
Various authors

ARABIAN HERITAGE GUIDES

Beachcombers' Guide to the Gulf
Tony Woodward

Off-Road in the Emirates
Dariush Zandi

Off-Road in the Emirates 2
Dariush Zandi

Off-Road in the Hejaz
Patrick Pierard and Patrick Legos

Off-Road in the Sultanate of Oman
Jenny Walker and Sam Owen

Reef Fishes UAE and Gulf of Oman
Richard Field

Snorkelling and Diving in Oman
Rod Salm and Robert Baldwin

The Off-Roaders Manual
Jehanbaz Ali Khan

Further titles are available. For a free books catalogue, call (+971 4) 282 4060 or fax (+971 4) 282 0428